ICL TEACHER'S/LEADER'S HANDBOOK

CREATIVE BIBLE LEARNING

FOR YOUNG CHILDREN
BIRTH-5 YEARS

BY DONNA HARRELL
AND WESLEY HAYSTEAD

INTERNATIONAL CENTER
FOR LEARNING
A Subsidiary of G/L Publications

© Copyright 1977 by Regal Books
All rights reserved

Fourth Printing, 1983

Published by Regal Books
A Division of GL Publications
Ventura, California 93006

Library of Congress Catalog Card No. 77-077030
ISBN 0-8307-0477-5

Contents

The Authors

Wesley Haystead is one of the five original team members of the International Center for Learning teaching staff and specializes in Early Childhood education. His teaching experience includes serving as a Minister of Christian Education and as a consultant in Children's Ministry. Wes received his Master's degree in Educational Psychology from the University of Southern California, Los Angeles. He manages and coordinates the Early Childhood and Children's teams for ICL. Wes also is the author of *You Can't Begin Too Soon.*

Donna Harrell graduated from Iowa State University in 1969, with a major in Child Development. Donna has been involved in many aspects of Early Childhood education. She has taught in a Headstart program and worked with handicapped children. As a Peace Corps volunteer, Donna worked in Costa Rica under the Ministry of Public Health in the field of child psychiatry. Donna has also been a Sunday School superintendent and has been involved in the training of teachers at the Early Childhood age level. Donna is currently the director of the Des Moines Christian Preschool and Day Care Center.

Foreword

The International Center for Learning is committed to obeying Christ's command to "Go...make disciples...and teach" (Matt. 28:19,20,*TLB*). To fulfill this great commission, ICL provides in-depth training for leaders ministering in churches of all sizes. ICL helps teachers discover how to motivate students to be involved in learning the life-changing truths of God's Word.

Since 1970, thousands of Sunday School teachers and leaders have attended ICL seminars and clinics. Repeatedly, teachers express a strong need for training, a desire to improve their abilities to teach God's Word. The response of these teachers to the ICL program has been enthusiastically positive.

This book is designed for both the new teacher and those who are more experienced. Wesley Haystead and Donna Harrell concisely present the needs and characteristics of young children. They will help you discover a variety of ways you can provide effective Bible learning. These insights into your learners, the learning process, and appropriate methods and materials will enable you to make the Bible come alive for your learners.

You can profit from reading this book and discussing it with a group of teachers. You will want to refer to this book many times for assistance in planning new methods and programs as well as improving what you are already doing. Also, consider using the book as a part of an ongoing training program for staff members in the Early Childhood Division of your church.

We trust that this book will help you as you obey Christ's command, "Go...make disciples...and teach."

Lowell E. Brown

Lowell E. Brown
Executive Director
International Center for Learning

Focus on Early Childhood

"Not now, dear. When you're older."
"That's for grownups, not children."
"Don't touch! You might break it."
How often have you heard these remarks spoken to a young child?! In a world of adults, young children often confront situations that make them feel incapable, insecure and sometimes unwanted. Similar comments were made by Jesus' followers when a group of children interrupted their discussion. But Jesus said, "Let the children alone, and do not hinder them from coming to Me; for the kingdom of heaven belongs to such as these" (Matt. 19:14).

Jesus commanded His followers not to turn away children who came to Him. Children have a place in His Kingdom. God loves infants as much as He loves adults, and toddlers as much as teenagers.

It is true that the first five years of life leave a child far short of adult understandings, skills and responsibilities. However, the child is still equipped with an amazing array of capacities that make thoughtful, loving ministry to him a necessity. Every teacher, parent, pastor and congregation that seriously wants to follow Jesus' example in the world must be concerned about children. A church must share Jesus' deep respect for a child, sensing the great value God places on each one.

WHY DO WE TEACH BIBLE TRUTHS TO YOUNG CHILDREN?

God's long-range goal for every child or adult is that he may "attain to the unity of the faith, and of the knowledge of the Son of God, to a mature man, to the measure of the stature which belongs to the fulness of Christ" (Eph. 4:13). The earliest beginnings of this great process can occur while the child is still a babe in arms, being loved by people who love God.

As the child grows, loving Christian adults work patiently in a wide variety of learning experiences, carefully introducing Bible truths that are appropriate for the child's level of development. Timothy was reminded that, as a child, he understood and responded to Bible truths, because these truths "make you wise to accept God's salvation by trusting in Christ Jesus. The whole Bible was given to us by inspiration from God and is useful to teach us what is true and to make us realize what is wrong in our lives; it straightens us out and helps us do what is right. It is God's way of making us well prepared at every point, fully equipped to do good to everyone" (2 Tim. 3:15-17, *TLB*).

Just as Timothy's boyhood introduction to Scripture began his preparation for a life of service, children today need the same opportunity, both at home and at church.

First, we teach the Bible to children in order that at God's appointed time, as the Holy Spirit guides, the child will express faith in the Lord Jesus Christ as Saviour, becoming a member of God's family. Jesus said, "You *must* be born again" (John 3:7, italics added).

But, like physical birth, this experience is part of a process. A baby must develop in the womb before he is born. Jesus compared the preparation of the heart to the planting of seed which later bears fruit. Ideas and attitudes that take root in the child will produce a rich harvest in years that follow. Most conversions among children are recorded between the ages of 10 and 12. However, the child who attends Sunday School during his early years—and particularly if from a supportive Christian home—often is capable of earlier response to Jesus' love. A child needs to be nurtured in the things of God in order to develop a personal faith.

Second, Bible truths appropriate to the child's development help in discerning right from wrong, building a foundation for truly Christian values. For example, the Bible command, "Be kind" (Eph. 4:32), takes on real meaning for a two-year-old when we help him to wait his turn to paint, and then praise him for obeying God's Word: "Waiting your turn to paint is a good way to 'be kind,' just like the Bible says." Children's values are formed by example and supported by words. The child constantly watches adult attitudes and actions. He desires to imitate the behavior of adults he admires. He seeks adult approval for that behavior. When he hears this behavior associated with Bible truth, it becomes even more important to him to continue that action. The process of connecting Bible statements to desired behaviors and attitudes is one important step in building a foundation for Christian values in a child's life.

Third, Bible truths help a child develop a biblical awareness of the world in which he lives. The child needs to feel that his own life and his world of people and experiences are all a part of God's loving plan and care. Children need the security that such a realization can bring. It was a moment of great wonder and comfort for Andrea when her teacher finished thanking God for the morning snack, then said, "God hears us when we talk to Him. He listens because He loves us. The Bible tells us 'God cares for you'" (1 Pet. 5:7, adapted from NASB). Such experiences bear fruit as the child's understanding is quickened by the Holy Spirit. If the child learns to believe in and count on God's unchanging love for him, he will learn to see himself as a person of worth.

Fourth, as the young child becomes familiar with ways Scriptures apply in his life, he develops a positive, receptive attitude to the Bible. The child learns that it is desirable to obey the commands of God and be strengthened by His promises.

Young children live in a world of immediacy. Their concern is with what is happening here and now. Teachers and parents who relate Bible truth to current experiences appeal to the child's need to find God at work in every area of life today.

HOW CAN WE TEACH BIBLE TRUTHS TO YOUNG CHILDREN?

Guiding children in their early years is an awesome task. The importance of helping children learn basic scriptural truth cannot be overemphasized. Fortunately, God has not left us alone to accomplish this task in our own strength. He offers us the instruction of the Holy Spirit and the promise of His guidance: "If you want to know what God wants you to do, ask him, and he will gladly tell you, for he is always ready to give a bountiful supply of wisdom to all who ask him; he will not resent it" (Jas. 1:5, *TLB*).

With this assurance of guidance how does one go about teaching little ones of God's love? What methods and techniques will communicate Bible truth in terms a child can understand?

The Christianity which we share must be more than a body of knowledge. It is not enough for the young child to hear God's Word or even to memorize it. He must *do* it. Direct, firsthand activity is the young child's most effective way to learn. He is not yet able to play with ideas; he must play with materials. He must use all of his senses—seeing, touching, tasting, smelling and hearing—in order to learn efficiently. Therefore, we are compelled to help him learn Bible truths through active play experiences. As the child paints or builds with blocks or tucks a doll in bed, a teacher can link those activities to Bible words and events, creating an effective learning experience out of what appears to be "just play."

Can your church provide an effective ministry to young children? Can you accept Jesus' concern for little ones? Do you have adults who want to share God's love to help children make a good beginning? The answer to those questions is not a matter of size, finances, programs or facilities. It is a matter of attitude and commitment. This handbook can help with ideas, with plans, with essential techniques. The help for attitudes and commitment can come only through earnest prayer.

Three stonemasons, when asked what they were doing, replied as follows:

"Laying a stone," said the first.

"Making a wall," said the second.

"Building a cathedral," said the third.

Three Sunday School teachers were asked what they were doing:

"Baby-sitting these kids," said the first.

"Caring for the children," said the second.

"Sharing God's love," replied the third.

Learning: A Process

When three-year-old Matthew's father mentioned that they were expecting friends to drop by that evening, Matthew enthusiastically asked if he could meet them at the door. "I want to tell them where they live!"

"But, Matt, you don't know where they live," his father responded.

"That's why I want to *tell* them where they live," said Matthew, totally unaware that the word he should have used was "ask," not "tell." Matthew was too busy with all the excitement of living to worry about the definitions of words. After all, he knew what he meant.

Yet, he also is anxious to make his intentions clear to his father. Thus, over a period of time, as Matthew talks with Dad and Mom and teachers and friends, he corrects his errors and becomes more efficient in communicating.

We call this process learning.

Learning is what Matthew is doing most of his waking hours. He is learning as he plays, as he struggles to tie his shoes, as he mixes yellow into his blue finger painting, as he rides his tricycle, as he asks questions. From dawn to dark he never stops learning information, skills and attitudes. He is learning who he is, and how he relates to people and things, and yes, to God.

WHAT DO WE WANT YOUNG CHILDREN TO LEARN?

"I want my child to learn about God and the Bible and Jesus!"

Eric was two, and his mother was concerned that he learn. But where do you start with a young child? What is most important for him to learn about God? What is he ready to understand about the Bible? Which stories about Jesus will have the most meaning to him now?

The basic learning that is fundamental to healthy development in a young child must involve not only what facts he understands, but what attitudes and behavior he displays. Many things are not understood by a child until they have been experienced many times. Knowledge, feelings and actions must be considered together in the child's learning. Grouping these experiences into six major areas is helpful for considering the basic learning that is achievable with children during the first five years of life:

Himself

Each child must develop positive feelings about himself. The child's attitude about himself will color his attitude about everyone else, every experience he has, and ultimately about God. His concept of himself is a mirror image of how he sees himself reflected in the actions of people around him. From infancy, the actions of parents and teachers show a child if he is a worthwhile individual, having value and ability.

Every young child needs to know he was made and is loved by God; that he is special, having abilities to do things that are significant; and that he is growing and learning as God planned for him.

This knowledge needs to be supported by *feelings* of love and security from experiences with parents, teachers, friends, and God. He needs to feel competent in tasks and situations that are presented him at church and at home.

The young child can *respond* by making suitable choices and meeting new situations confidently; by displaying independence appropriate to his age level; by talking with teachers and friends; by expressing feelings openly; by working successfully at tasks appropriate to his development.

Others

From infancy the child's world centers on his own needs and desires. A baby's initial interest in people centers on their role in satisfying his demands. As he grows, he begins to identify and appreciate others, first in his family, and then beyond the family circle. The child begins to love others only as he has been loved. He learns to respect others as he has been respected. Positive interactions with family, friends and teachers provide a foundation on which understanding and feelings about others begin to grow.

A young child can *know* that God made and loves everyone; that God wants him to show love and kindness to others; and that God has provided many other people—families, teachers, friends—who love and help him.

A child needs to *feel* accepted by his family and friends; love toward specific people he knows; interest and respect for others; and a desire to help and assist when needed.

The child can *respond* by respecting the rights of others; by showing love for others through helping, sharing and taking turns; and by participating in group activities.

Church

The child thinks of the church in terms of a building. With thoughtful guidance by parents and teachers he can begin to think of the church as people, people who love God and come together to worship. Avoid using the term "God's house" with young children, for their literal minds will invariably conclude God lives inside the building.

Help the child *know* that church people come together to learn about God and Jesus; that they sing and pray because they love God; and that his room at church has been planned for him and his friends.

Thoughtful teachers are essential to help a child *feel* loved and accepted by people at church; comfortable and happy in his room at church; and a desire to come to church.

Appropriate *responses* by young children include: listening carefully, singing, praying, bringing love gifts, being helpful by working and playing cooperatively; caring for the church building, equipment and materials; and relating to teachers as facilitators, sources of assistance and models of Christian behavior.

Bible and Prayer

The Bible and prayer both have a mysterious attraction to young children. While there is much about both that the child does not comprehend, there are some basic understandings and attitudes that are important to develop about these two means of communication between God and us.

The child should *know* that the Bible is a special book which tells about God and Jesus; that Bible stories are true; that the Bible provides help in knowing what is the best thing to do; that he can talk to God about the things that interest him; and that he can pray at any time.

Pleasant experiences with the Bible and prayer will help the child *feel* a desire to hear Bible stories; assurance that Bible commands are helpful for him; and confidence that God hears his prayers.

A child can *respond* by listening to and talking about Bible stories; by demonstrating ways to obey specific Bible commands; by handling the Bible carefully; and by talking to God in various situations.

Jesus

Young children are easily attracted to Jesus. He is seen as a warm, sympathetic person who likes children, therefore children like Him. These early feelings form the foundation for receiving Jesus as Saviour and following His example in Christian living.

The child can be led to know that Jesus was born as a baby, grew to be a child and then a man; that He did kind, loving things; that He taught people about God; that He was God's special Son; that He died, being punished for the wrong things we have done; and that He rose from the dead and is still alive.

Expect children to feel love for Jesus; gratitude for His kindness; and a desire to do things that Jesus did.

Children may respond by singing songs about Jesus; listening to and talking about stories of Jesus; and demonstrating behavior in imitation of Jesus. Some children may respond by praying to become a member of God's family, accepting Jesus as Saviour. Expect wide variations in children's readiness to understand the meaning of becoming a Christian. Some children with a strong Christian background may be ready to accept Christ in early childhood, but the child without such support will usually need additional years of instruction and interaction.

God

As teachers demonstrate love to a child while talking to him about God's love, a concept which is abstract begins to take on some concrete form in the child's mind. Not being able to see or touch God, the child is totally dependent on what he sees in the lives of significant adults. In a very real sense, parents and teachers are like God to the child.

The child needs to know that God made all things and that God cares for him; that God knows what is best for him to do; and that God forgives him when he is sorry for doing something wrong.

The child can be helped to feel loved by God; thankful for God's love and care; and a desire to obey God's commands.

The child can *respond* by demonstrating joy and thankfulness in prayer, song and conversation; by naming ways God cares for him; and by demonstrating ways that show obedience to God.

Most formal teaching efforts focus on the things adults want children to *know*. While accurate information is important, the child's attitudes and behavior will have more impact on the kind of person he is becoming. Teachers who want to see long-term results for their efforts must give considerable attention to all dimensions of a child's learning, not being satisfied to merely communicate facts.

HOW DO CHILDREN ACQUIRE INFORMATION AND ATTITUDES?

How do you learn? How do you acquire information or develop opinions? Perhaps by reading books? By listening to a lecture or sermon, by watching a film or television program? By discussion with someone else? Much adult learning is by means of *words*, symbols by which we are able to communicate.

Learning in early childhood is different from learning as an adult, however. The mind of the child is not capable of handling ideas coming in words only. The young child does not have the ability to give real meaning to a "flat" word unless it is a very familiar part of his experience and will evoke ideas and feelings from his memory.

Through the Senses

While we cannot know all that occurs in the mind of a young child, we do know that information enters his mind through the gates of the senses—seeing, feeling, smelling, tasting and hearing. The learning experience begins as a *sensory* process.

Firsthand experiences are the hard core of learning for young children, and these experiences all relate to one or more of the senses. The program which enables learning to take place must have this understanding as its basis. Activities at Sunday School must involve as many of the child's five senses as possible.

When two-year-old Debbie pleaded, "Let me see it!" she really meant, "Let me feel it, touch it, shake it, put it in my mouth, rub it against my cheek and take a deep breath to see how it smells!" Through the senses the child learns of God's world and the people in it. As you plan learning activities for young children, ask yourself, "How many senses will they use as they participate in these experiences?"

For example, a very satisfactory sensory experience is that of eating an apple. God has made apples in a way that appeals to all of the senses. They are bright red or green, or else their color is delicately shaded. Their shape is round, fitting securely into the hand. The firmness of the fruit makes touching them a joy. They can be rolled around in the hand. Their aroma causes digestive juices to run. Their taste is delicate but distinctive, and their crunch as one bites into them is unmistakable. Eating an apple is a total sensory experience which is unforgettable to the child and will enrich his memories for the rest of his life.

Try offering a child a piece of apple to taste. Then, when he smiles at the flavor, ask, "Would you like to thank God for apples?" The resulting one-sentence prayer will be spoken with genuine thanksgiving.

By Repetition

The activities you offer need not change every week. In fact, they *should* not. If a child feels happy and satisfied with his learning experience he will want to repeat it. Repetition is a necessary (and natural) part of a child's learning. Songs and stories become favorites only when they are enjoyed over and over.

While Steve and Ellen were building with blocks, Miss Cowen began to sing, "Who made Steve's hands? Who made Ellen's hands? God made Steve's hands, and, God made Ellen's hands." Later, during Together Time, the whole department sang, "Who made my hands?" Throughout the morning the song was sung during various activities. On the way home, Steve grandly announced, "I know a song about Steve's hands!"

By Multiple Varied Experiences

A teacher's planning must provide variety, also. Children need new experiences as well as opportunities to repeat their learning in different ways. For example, a child will have difficulty knowing how to be kind, helpful and loving unless he has many different experiences where the words are used to identify his actions, and those of teachers and friends.

While the "Good Samaritan" is an action-packed narrative, a story is not the only way to teach being kind. The point of a story is most clearly understood when it is told after children have had opportunity to practice the behavior mentioned.

The Sunday Mrs. Evers told the Good Samaritan story, she had the children make Get Well cards at the art table to practice an act of kindness. At the same time, Mr. Tucker was showing some other children how to be kind to the guinea pig in the God's Wonders center. Mrs. Lucas was acting out a visit to the doctor with some of the children in the Home Living corner, enabling them to see the doctor as a kind helper who cares for them. Later, when Mr. Tucker told the Bible story to his class, he reminded them of ways he had seen them help that morning, "just like the kind man in our story."

By Practice in Play

The child also needs opportunities to practice through firsthand experiences that have a meaning for him in everyday life. The repetition of firsthand experiences strengthens habits, attitudes, knowledge and understanding that reflect Christian values. For this reason teachers need to plan learning activities which incorporate such skills as problem solving, getting along with other children, listening and speaking, and roleplaying. Conversation using Bible verses should be directly connected with the activities. Children learn because they are *doing*. And for young children, doing is play.

Play does not sound very educational—or spiritual. But play is a child's full-time occupation: it is the activity through which he learns best. In the adult world a distinction is often made between work and play. Not so in the world of young children! For the young child the time given to play is just as significant, demanding and exhausting as the time his parents spend at work or in managing the home. Blocks, dolls, puzzles and paints are the tools children use in play. They are tools by which children can learn.

By Imitation

The teacher's example is a vital part of a young child's learning. Much of the way in which the child will go about doing—his style or approach to materials—he will pick up from his teachers and parents. Guiding play, therefore, means *participating* in play. The teacher who wants young children to enjoy the emotional release of pounding clay must sit with the children and join in. The teacher who has children roleplay kindness to babies cannot then toss the doll in the corner as she leaves the play area. Rather she must carefully and lovingly place the doll in its cradle. In this way she provides a pattern for the child, a model to be copied.

By Connecting Words to Actions

Words are the building blocks of thoughts. We must have words to define the concepts we use in thinking. Children have limited vocabularies and experience. This combination results in a limited ability to manipulate concepts. When the Christian adult takes a bite of apple, he may think to himself, "That tastes good! I'm glad God made apples!" The young child, however, may only think, "Mmm!" The adult teacher must provide words for him, helping him to identify his response to the experience, and relating God to the event. Once this relationship is made, the child is able to think about God, or Jesus, or the Bible words he heard, the next time he eats something good. Without such adult guidance the experience would be simply another of many taste sensations to be stored for later reference.

HOW DO CHILDREN PROCESS INFORMATION?

According to Past Experience

The information entering by the gateway of the senses is processed by the child's mind in ways unique to himself. All his experiences, at home, at church, at nursery school, are the basis for his processing of the information you are trying to communicate to him.

Brian has been successful in the past at cutting, so he may choose that activity eagerly. He will listen to your directions, relate your words to previous encounters with scissors, and be eager to get to work. He will be able to talk with you about the pictures he is cutting. However, Molly has had difficulty with scissors in the past, and may come with some reluctance. She may not be capable of following your directions. She may not respond at all to conversation about the pictures because she is too busy concentrating on cutting to hear what you say.

Experiences also shape attitudes. An alert teacher can help a child build positive attitudes by working with the child to insure success. Molly's teacher quickly saw her difficulty. "Molly, I'll hold the paper while you cut it." At each laborious stroke of the scissors, the teacher praised Molly's effort. No mention was made of missing the line. The important thing was that Molly was cutting! Gradually, Molly's attitude changed from defeat and frustration to positive confidence that she could cut. This was due to the teacher giving just enough help so that Molly could succeed, then praising her efforts. Teachers need to observe carefully individual children's abilities, then structure activities in such a way that all the children can succeed. Activities must be flexible enough to challenge those whose skills are more developed. The child's estimate of his own success will be his basis for his attitude in later experiences.

From a Self-centered Viewpoint

The young child's thinking automatically focuses on himself

rather than others. He blindly assumes that everybody else perceives and interprets things exactly as he does. A toddler dramatically demonstrates this quality when he attempts to hide himself during a game of hide-and-seek by standing in the middle of the floor and tightly closing his eyes. His assumption is that if he cannot see others, they cannot see him!

The three-year-old who stands up to get a better look is not concerned that children behind him now cannot see at all. This self-centered approach to the world is often annoying, but normal at this stage. The child needs adults to give gentle guidance in dealing with the inevitable conflicts caused by this limited viewpoint.

The child needs many opportunities to interact with others, in order to begin recognizing other points of view. Imaginative play is one of the best devices the child has for this learning. When Carol was playing "mother," her dealings with her "children" gave her a new understanding of how her own mother thinks and feels.

With Concrete Interpretations

Because the child learns through physical experiences with people and things, his thinking processes also focus on that which is concrete and tangible. Symbolism and abstractions that convey great meaning to adults usually communicate little to a child, for he interprets them literally. Sometimes this creates comic results, as with six-year-old Stephanie who announced that Jesus got into her heart by "sliding down my tongue." Deeper thought about her remark removed the humor, however, when teachers realized that the practice of referring to "Jesus in my heart" had led her to visualize only a tiny figure of a man sitting somewhere inside her chest.

Implications of These Factors

It is important to understand these factors that influence a child's thinking, so that materials and methods can be appropriately chosen to accomplish meaningful learning. Because the young child interprets experiences on the basis of past success or failure, because he views the world from a very self-centered perspective, and because he interprets information concretely, the best approach with the child is to provide many activities in which he can succeed, to structure opportunities for imaginative play and interaction, and to carefully present information avoiding symbolism and abstraction.

WHAT NEEDS AFFECT THE PROCESS?

Every child has specific, personal needs that mark him as a unique individual. There are, also, basic needs which are common to all children. Since these needs obviously influence the children's learning, it is important to take note of them.

Physical Needs

These are usually fairly obvious and include such needs as physical activity, rest, food, water and touch. Until the physical needs are met, the child is not able to give energy and attention to learning. Subsequent chapters deal in greater detail with many of these needs at specific age levels.

Safety and Security

Part of an adult's responsibility is to guard the physical and emotional safety of children. First, we must protect them from physical harm. To prevent accidents, be alert for potentially dangerous situations. Check toys and other equipment regularly for sharp points and edges. Be sure furniture is sturdy, free from splinters and sharp corners.

Be alert for the child who does not feel well. Help parents be aware of the need for enforcing sensible health and safety regulations to protect all the children. A child who is ill should always be kept at home.

We must also protect children from emotional harm. Accept

their emotional needs and be ready to help meet them. Fear, anger, loneliness and frustration are common emotions, for which children need understanding adults to help them cope. Never ridicule or shame them. Help them feel secure in your love and protection.

You see a child stepping into your room on Sunday, but he is really stepping out. He is taking important steps toward independence and finding himself as a person. Coming to Sunday School may be the first time he moves beyond the circle of his family, unless he already attends nursery school. The child needs to know that while he may reach out for new and exciting adventures, he can depend upon familiar and comforting adults.

The child finds security in familiar surroundings and procedures. Plan a program that follows the same general routine every session. Supply basic equipment that will be available to the child every Sunday, for he enjoys using the same toys again and again. Repeat Bible stories and sing familiar songs throughout each week of a unit.

The young child also finds security in limits. He needs to know what is expected of him, what he can and cannot do. Establishing limits to insure children's physical safety is your first consideration. (For instance, no child may leave the room alone.) Also set limits for the appropriate use of equipment and materials. For example, puzzle pieces must be kept on the table; blocks remain in the building area; Home Living area equipment must not be stepped on. Allow as much freedom as possible within these limits, but be consistent. The same procedures for use of blocks should be followed during Sunday School, Church Time and any other occasion when blocks are used. When you remind a child of the limits, it helps to phrase your words positively. "We keep puzzle pieces on the table," rather than, "Don't carry away the puzzle pieces."

Positive relationships with loving Christian adults contribute greatly to the development of trust in the life of the child. One way a child will often express his trust in an adult is by asking questions: "Where does my shadow go at night?" "Why is it raining?" "Are you my friend?" "Where is Jesus?"...

A child's questions are among his highest compliments, for in asking them he is extending himself in an act of trust. It is this trust that is the foundation for faith in God. God uses parents and teachers to provide the initial security that prepares the child to understand God's faithfulness in caring for the child.

Love and Acceptance

Knowing and feeling he is loved is essential to a child's feeling of security. Both words and actions show that you love him, that he is important. He must experience your love in order to begin to understand God's love. When he feels secure and comfortable in your love he will begin to feel secure in God's love.

The Lord said, "I have loved you with an everlasting love" (Jer. 31:3). All people need love that is unconditional and ever available. Christ offers this to us and we must express it to the child. Love that does not depend on circumstances or behavior offers a child opportunity for growth and development in all areas of his life.

Your helpful actions, your smile, even your tone of voice can say, "I love you." For one child a smile across the room or a friendly pat on the shoulder is enough to let him know he is important to you. For another it takes a hug or a few minutes of cuddling to let him know he is special.

Offer honest, specific praise when a child does something positive. Listen to the child when he speaks to you and use his name often as you talk with him. Bend down to his eye level to show your genuine interest in what he has to tell you. Send a card or telephone a child occasionally. Let him know how happy you are to see him each week.

A child understands God's love as he experiences love from understanding adults. He needs to see love in the attitudes and actions of his teachers and other adults who love God. You are Christ's letter "written not with ink, but with the Spirit of the living God, not on tablets of stone, but on tablets of human hearts" (2 Cor. 3:3).

A child's feeling that he is loved is the foundation on which he builds love toward others. He learns to love by being loved. As he has continuing opportunities to love and to be loved, love can become a part of his pattern of living.

Usually, the child who seems the least lovable is the one who needs love the most. Pray for that child and ask God to show love to him through you. Help him feel loved and accepted regardless of what he does or does not do.

Acceptance is not the same thing as approval. Acceptance means recognizing a child's feelings without blaming, but it does not mean permitting the child to demonstrate unacceptable behavior. When a child exhibits feelings of anger or unfriendliness, accept the child even though you do not approve of his actions. Gently enforce the limits which have been established and safeguard the rights of all children.

For instance, when Scott, with a scowl on his face, comes to the block building area and deliberately kicks over Sharon's construction, an initial reaction might be to say, "Stop that! You're a bad boy!" However, the thoughtful teacher might put her hand on Scott's shoulder, guide him away from the area and say, "Scott, I know you're angry right now. But I cannot let you knock down Sharon's blocks." The teacher recognizes Scott's angry feelings, and talks with him about those feelings. To help Scott bring his feelings under control, the teacher might guide him to a table activity where he can work with an understanding adult nearby. "Here is some dough to work with. Mr. Hardy has Popsicle sticks for you to cut the dough." The teacher then returns to the block building area to clarify Scott's actions and help restore Sharon's feelings. "Scott was feeling angry. I am sorry he kicked over your building. When he feels happy again he can work with his friends."

In order to accept a child, you must first understand him. How well do you know each child in your class? Observe each one thoughtfully; and listen to their chatter as they play. Arrange to meet the parents, asking them for suggestions on ways to meet their child's interests and needs. Learning to understand each child will provide a sound basis for loving acceptance of him.

Esteem

Recognition of the child's worth goes hand in hand with providing love and acceptance. Consider how important every individual is to God. Jesus said that no sparrow can fall to the ground without God's knowledge; yet each of us is worth more to God than any sparrow. The child needs to know that God knows all about him and loves him very much.

It is from our model, Jesus Christ, that we have learned to respect young children. He demonstrated their importance to Him when He interrupted a sermon for adults to hold small children on his lap. Jesus clearly recognized the dignity and value of the young child. He saw little ones not just as potential adults, but as people already possessing unique qualities and personal worth.

Treat the child with respect. Sometimes adults neglect to show a young child respect because they forget that he, too, is a person. Never shame him. Avoid labeling him a "bad boy" or a "baby." Avoid talking about a child with other adults when the child is present. Give the child a few minutes notice before ending an activity he is enjoying. Be realistic and consistent in your expectations for the child's behavior, being firm and loving when correction is necessary. Extend to him the common courtesies you would show an adult friend. Even hearing "please," "thank you," "excuse me," or "I'm sorry" will help the child feel he is a worthwhile person.

Development of Personal Potential

The child needs to develop his potential in every area—physical skills, intellectual understanding, social interaction, emotional expression and spiritual insight. Our responsibility is to help each child develop, at his own rate, to be the best he can be for God in every area of his life and personality at any given time.

A child is not born with the ability to control his own actions. He must develop self-control with the careful guidance of adults he trusts. Developing this self-control does not happen overnight. It takes time. A child first needs to know what adults expect of him. After he has tested these limits and found them to be consistent, he can begin to develop his own system of self-control. By adhering to a well-organized routine and enforcing a few rules of conduct, adults encourage the child in his efforts to be responsible for his own actions. From this responsibility grows self-control—discipline from within.

The young child's "Let me do it!" is evidence of his first steps toward self-control and independence. He is attempting to discover his own abilities. He needs to know he can do things on his own, but with the assurance there is an understanding teacher nearby on whom he can depend if he needs assistance.

Careful, thoughtful guidance is needed to help the child develop competence in a world built for people more than twice his size. In his room at church, give him freedom in choosing materials and activities. Materials should be readily accessible. Arrange them so the child knows where they are, can reach what he requires without asking for assistance and return them when he is through.

Give the child as much independence as he can handle. Encourage his efforts and praise his accomplishments. Let him do as much as possible on his own. When it is necessary to assist, give suggestions that will enable the child to experience success, not just sit and watch you complete the activity.

For example, "Do you think the puzzle piece will fit if you turn it around?" or "It might be easier for you to hang up your coat if I hold the hanger very still." As the child experiences success in using his rapidly developing skill, his confidence grows and he is encouraged to attempt more challenging endeavors.

As we meet these basic needs of children we begin to free them to learn. They are able to concentrate on the new experiences and information we offer them.

HOW DOES ABILITY AFFECT THE PROCESS?

Every child is a unique miracle of God's making. From the time of his birth each one is different from all others—God planned it so. Individual differences are apparent in even the youngest babies.

Most Sunday School teachers prepare for the "average" child. Since almost every child is outside the "average" range for his age group in some area of development, there is great need for teachers to be flexible in lesson planning. This need is intensified whenever there is a child in the group who is significantly different from most of the other children.

Expect young children to respond in many different ways to any given activity. For example, one teacher prepared an activity for children to paste magazine pictures of people God made. One boy was only interested in the pasting, taking whatever picture was on top of the pile and laboriously adding it to his page which became covered with pictures. Next to him were two girls who took great pains to find particular kinds of people. Across the table was a boy who wanted to write the "names" below his pictures. And then there was a girl who quickly pasted two pictures, announced she was done, and hurried over to the Home Living area! All were happy with what they were doing, for they were encouraged to work at their own level.

Jimmy was a gifted child who often caused a disturbance in the room. His teachers began giving Jimmy extra personal attention. They discussed ways each activity could be stretched to make it more challenging for him. He was made responsible for jobs and was given recognition for his positive actions. Eventually, Jimmy could participate happily, for his unique needs were being met. Instead of trying to pressure Jimmy into doing everything the same as others, his teachers challenged him, making him feel accepted within the Christian community.

Angel was a little girl who was a slow learner. Physically she was developing normally, but she was not as quick to grasp new ideas as her peers. Her Sunday School teachers made a commitment to provide normal learning experiences at her own pace for Angel. For example, her attention span was very short. When she lost interest in the Bible story, the department leader would invite her to look at a book—and would provide her the same learning on a personal basis. She was thus able to grow without being deprived of those early learning experiences which are so important for mental development. Had Angel simply been "left out" because she was unable to keep up with others her age, her likelihood of normal development would have been much more limited. Today Angel is still a slow learner, but she has become a good group member and is loved by all those she is around. Her abilities also seem to be increasing beyond what was expected.

It is important that we remember that every part of the Body of Christ is important and significant. Intelligence and abilities are not God's standard for assessing spirituality. God does not ask us our IQ. His measure is love.

Learning About Children

Each child is a part of God's ongoing act of creation. God is the initiator of both the natural and spiritual birth of His children. Each child has a purpose in life, a potential that can only be dreamed of by the adults who know him. Each child is an individual, with capabilities and purposes unique to him. While each child must progress through common growth stages, each does so at his own pace and with his own style.

THE CHILD FROM BIRTH TO SIX MONTHS

Physical Development

Observe a child through the first six months of life. You will see him change from a little bundle which makes only reflexive grasping motions and sleeps nearly 20 hours a day, to a baby who is able to lift his head and probably his chest off the mattress, sit up with support, grab purposefully at hanging toys and perhaps hold his own bottle.

Most children up to the age of six months will remain in one place, although by the end of that period some are becoming mobile. The baby's physical development during this period is tremendous but is sometimes overlooked because he continues to be extremely dependent. He must rely on someone else to take care of all his physical comfort needs from feeding, to changing, to turning him over in his crib.

Facilities and Equipment

Facilities for baby care at church must accommodate all of the young child's needs. Infants need a place where they are safe from the probing fingers of older babies and toddlers, preferably in a room of their own with equipment designed for their age. (See chapter 6 for details.)

Social Development

A baby is more responsive to people than to anything else in his environment. A newborn quickly uses his eyes to establish contact. Smiles become common around two months. Always, he is sensitive to the moods of those around him.

A Sunday School teacher desiring to build good attitudes should gently approach the baby, making soft, soothing sounds. Hold the baby; reassure him and make him comfortable. This causes him to feel that he is in a safe, warm environment. Consistently reflect God's love as you feed and change him. Show the child you are glad to do this for him to make him comfortable. Even infants are quick to sense any displeasure you have in changing their diapers.

Ask parents for the baby's feeding schedule in writing. Then follow it exactly. Feed, burp and rock baby without rushing. Humming and soft singing help him back to sleep.

The attitude in which his needs are met now will greatly influence his developing personality and approach to the world. For instance, the child whose needs are lovingly met as soon as he cries, begins to realize that he can affect his environment and situation. A consistent pattern of warm attention will encourage him to trust people and have a confident approach to life. Children who are ignored and left to cry for long periods have been observed to become less and less communicative, as if they realize that efforts at communication are useless.

Sing-song rhymes and simple songs are a natural kind of conversation with babies. Singing and humming provide soothing sounds that contribute to a peaceful atmosphere. Babies soon begin to respond to favorites, such as "Jesus Loves Me," and "Bye-Low, My Baby,"[1] when they hear them over and over again.

During these first months the baby develops a social personality. He grows to know his regular nursery teacher. He learns to relax when friendly, loving hands support and cuddle him. This makes it imperative that a staff of regular workers be maintained so that the little ones can begin to identify with their "friend at church."

Crying

All babies cry, but there are great variations from baby to baby. Some babies cry more readily and more intensely than others. When a baby cries hard he pulls up his legs, and tightens every muscle. The face turns red and the arms wave about. Crying is the only way the baby can tell you when he is hungry, uncomfortable or frightened.

As you work with a baby on a regular basis you learn to distinguish one cry from another. There is usually a difference in tone and pitch between his hunger cry, the fretting cry, and the cry of pain or discomfort. Careful observation as a nursery teacher will help you to gain this awareness.

Regardless of your ability to distinguish cries, make sure your assumptions are right by investigating thoroughly. Be sure he is as comfortable as you can make him. Try burping him as it may be gas that is making him uncomfortable. Or, if his mother has sent a bottle, check whether he is hungry by offering him the bottle. Perhaps he has a wet or soiled diaper; investigate and change him if necessary.

Make sure you have some sort of system for checking diapers. A mimeographed attendance chart to which names can be added each Sunday can be checked as you change each baby. This will help you see that the quiet, resting babies also are checked for wet or soiled diapers during the occasional quiet moments.

Once you have done everything you can to make the baby comfortable, he is usually better off by himself. If he continues to cry he may need to be held and comforted. It is unlikely you will "spoil" a baby by holding him during the one or two hours a week he is with you.

Your attitude toward the child and his behavior is always the key. Your calm and gentle voice helps babies feel reassured long before they understand your words. Avoid babytalk. Use short simple sentences with words that mean exactly what they say. "I love Tommy. God loves Tommy." As the teacher cuddles Tommy and smiles warmly, Tommy begins to associate the word "God" with a pleasant experience.

Security-seeking Behaviors

Other behaviors which cause teachers some anxiety are those which the child uses to give him security, such as thumb-sucking, blanket carrying, and banging or rocking. Each of these behaviors is perfectly normal in the infant. Their behaviors manifest themselves frequently under stress or tension or before the baby goes to sleep. Therefore, the teacher's calm acceptance of the child in the face of these behaviors will go a long way toward helping the child to overcome them.

Studies have shown that many healthy babies enjoy sucking their thumbs even though they are not fatigued, hungry or uncomfortable. Thumb-sucking in most babies ceases eventually if undue attention is not paid to it.

Blanket carrying is another behavior that infants and young children exhibit frequently. For some reason, the child derives great comfort and security from holding his old rag or a particular soft toy and doesn't want to part with it for even a few hours. He tucks it under his arm and constantly rubs it between his fingers or under his nose while sucking his thumb. This, too, he will eventually give up as he matures.

Some babies bump their heads against the crib or rock from side to side instead of sucking their thumbs. This is the same type of rhythmic activity as thumb-sucking. Even though you may think the baby is hitting his head very hard, he can't do much damage, but you may provide cribs with four-sided bumper pads to soften the blows.

Intellectual Growth

Learning begins the minute the baby begins to record observations about his environment in his brain. This may well occur before his birth.

You can aid in this development by providing stimulations for his senses. A baby who cries for no apparent reason may simply be bored and will respond positively to colorful things to see and new sounds to hear. A crib mobile will provide something interesting to look at while he is in the lying and watching stage. When he begins to reach for things and tries to grasp them, it is time to place one or two bright toys within his reach. A small rattle or a brightly colored fabric doll which he can easily hold will be just right. (All toys should be washable and should be sterilized after every session.) Hang toys by strings from a piece of elastic stretched across the crib or playpen. This will save you steps and the baby will learn to grab the toys as he wants them. The elastic will help the toys move or react to the baby's movement and he will soon be able to pull the toys closer to him.

Babies quickly develop the knack of putting everything they find into their mouths. This is an essential part of their learning but can also be dangerous. Check the floor carefully on Sunday morning before the infants arrive and pick up any items that may have been dropped. Small buttons or pins may not be easily noticed but will be found by the infant who is becoming mobile.

Milestones of Development

Listed on the next page are some behaviors you may observe in the infant from birth to six months. Each child is unique and will follow this pattern at his own rate and may skip some behaviors or not develop them until later.

By the time he is three months old the baby may:
hold his head well off the bed when he's placed on his abdomen;
smile in response to your voice;
follow a moving person or object with his eyes;
stare at a bright object;
turn head to voice or familiar sound.

Between the time he is three and four months old the baby may:
begin to grasp a toy in his hand; push himself up on his arms;
coo and gurgle with pleasure;
roll from his back to his side;
be quieted by a voice or by music;
begin to play with his hands;
turn his head freely to watch activities and objects around him;
smile and respond to friendly overtures;
hold his head erect;
vocalize, cough or click his tongue to initiate "conversation."

Between the time he is four and six months old the baby may:
Laugh out loud;
hold his toys;
wave his hands to be lifted;
reach for objects;
make noise when he hears a voice;
lift head and shoulders and roll over;
roll from his back to his stomach;
sit up with some propping.

THE CHILD FROM SIX MONTHS TO EIGHTEEN MONTHS

Physical Development

During the child's second half year, changes come almost faster than we can chart them. His ability to move around increases almost daily. He crawls actively and sits upright for a period of time. The first teeth begin to come in and solid food is added to his diet. The creeper explores the world with his mouth—biting and tasting everything within his grasp. He grabs a toy in the crib, drops it, bangs his fist in protest, cries and then repeats the sequence all over again. After he learns to pinch his thumb and forefinger together, he tries to hold his bottle and feed himself.

The ability to spend time "sitting up" means the baby is ready for a whole series of new experiences. Both hands are free to manipulate toys and to hold books and pictures for close inspection. Often you will notice that a baby's hands and feet are his favorite toys and are always available.

The baby who is already a creeper pulls himself up on furniture and stands alone. He exerts his independence by crawling away, resisting dressing, refusing a bottle, kicking and screaming. As the child nears his first birthday, he can walk holding onto furniture and may take his first independent step.

After he gains confidence in his standing ability, he will begin to take a few tentative steps, still holding on to the furniture or playpen rail. Don't urge him at this point. Let him take his time, and somewhere between the twelfth and fifteenth month, he'll probably take off on his own.

Once a child has left his crib for crawling or walking experiences, safety measures are a vital consideration. Check equipment for sharp edges, loose pieces, cleanliness, chipping paint or any other potential safety hazard. Also check doors, windows or any openings through which a child might venture. Equip electric outlets with safety covers.

Facilities and Equipment

The room should be equipped with a few cribs for those babies who will need to nap. Because older babies want to move about, provide ample floor space. See chapter 6 for details.

Mental and Emotional Development

At about six months the infant often quite suddenly becomes shy and afraid of strangers. A child who has previously been quite happy in the church nursery may begin to cry when his mother leaves now. Perhaps it is because he begins to see himself as a separate person. A newborn cannot differentiate between his own body and the rest of the world. Then he slowly begins to learn about himself as an individual. Crying at this point is definitely a step of progress.

Sometime during this year, a baby discovers that he has a mind of his own, and wants to exercise it. One evidence of this growth is when he resists your efforts to get him to do things. He also becomes more and more energetic and, in his urge to explore, will be "into everything."

Babies want to touch and handle everything they see. Sometimes, for their own safety, you will have to hold them back. Avoid unnecessarily limiting this growing desire to explore, however, since investigation is the best way children have to familiarize themselves with the world about them. When an interesting activity must be curtailed, a child may feel frustrated and then become angry.

When a child displays anger, the teacher may feel a bit angry, too. However, gentle calm teachers will generally have a quieting effect on the baby.

The happiest and most wisely handled child in the world may have occasional temper tantrums. Walking away from a child in a tantrum may calm him down. Usually he will stop screaming when he finds you're not there to watch him. Children also have tantrums when they're tired, overstimulated, or ordered about too much.

Good discipline begins with a consistent attitude. If you allow the children to do something one day, you can't expect them to understand why you try to stop them from doing it again. But if they are sure of your love for them, they will be able to take limitations when they are necessary.

Try to anticipate a baby's desire. For example, lift him out of a crib before he tires of it, so he won't get the idea that he's getting his way by crying. Be patient with him.

Play

Play occupies an increasingly large place in the child's life. A child plays spontaneously. You don't have to teach him how to play or provide him with special toys. The urge comes from within.

A child learns, develops and builds knowledge through play. Play reflects children's understanding of the world and is therefore a constant testing of the world. Most of a child's play is alone or with an adult. He enjoys peek-a-boo and simple hide-and-seek as long as he can be found quickly.

When a child begins to explore the world by creeping and walking, he will enjoy the companionship of youngsters somewhere near his own age.

At this stage children will not play cooperatively. They will show an interest in each other, but each will play with his own toys for short periods of time. There will be few squabbles because each is too absorbed in his own play to worry about what his companion may be doing.

Select those toys which will allow a child to express his own creativity and imagination. A child this age will enjoy large, colorful toys with movable parts he can manipulate. He will enjoy putting things together, such as placing one empty box in another, or fitting pans inside other pans. He will also like to fit pegs of various shapes into their proper holes on a board.

The toys should be stored in a toy cupboard or on shelves low enough for the children to reach, rather than in a bin where they become jumbled and often broken.

Verbal Ability

The child enjoys hearing simple conversation and songs. He begins to imitate sounds and learns to distinguish the tone of voice of the people around him. Around the time of his first birthday he says his first word. Sometimes this first word will go completely unnoticed for a while simply because it doesn't sound like the word the baby is trying to imitate. But after he has used a certain sound several times to indicate a certain thing, adults catch on to what he's trying to say.

Usually the first thing that the baby will say is "da-da-da." He'll also learn to use "bye-bye" and wave along with it. Later in this period, before reaching 12 months, the baby usually says "mama."

Many babies will not "perform" for strangers and so, although they may be using a few words at home, they will probably not use them in the nursery at first.

The baby may also stop adding words to his vocabulary for a while after his first two or three are understood. There may be a halt, too, while he is learning to walk, but he will make up for lost time after he has become an accomplished walker. In the meantime, help the child add to his listening and understanding vocabulary by talking to him in short, simple words. Sing nursery songs and recite rhymes. A few very simple finger plays and sentences can be introduced at this stage also. Do not talk too fast, though, and keep sentences short and simple.

Encourage children in their efforts to talk. Avoid the temptation to mimic baby talk. Babies learn by imitating the way adults talk. If you reverse the procedure and adopt their way of saying things, they will not be given the opportunity to learn the right way. Do not try to make children change the way they pronounce words, however. Just say the words they use clearly and correctly each time you use them. Also, respond to baby's babbling with clear statements. For instance, a child struggling to pull a teddy bear through the bars of a playpen may be frustratedly saying, "Doo-doo! Doo-doo!" As you help him, say "Here's the teddy bear."

Milestones of Development

Having discussed infant stages from 6 to 18 months, the following lists may help you as you observe the babies you are teaching in the nursery.

Between the ages of six and eight months the baby may:
object noisily when an object is taken away from him;
recover a rattle if it falls within easy reach;
reach for paper;
cough artificially and know he's cute;
discriminate between a stranger and a familiar person;

Between the ages of 8 and 12 months the baby may:
sit up well without support;
bang spoon or pat table in play;
be more active with a little help;
pick up a cube or block off the table, or
hold a block in each hand;
show his temper if he is frustrated or thwarted;
show pleasure by cooing or crowing;

Between the ages of 12 and 18 months the baby may:
walk alone or with a little help;
lower himself from a standing to sitting position;
repeat his actions if laughed at;
blow bubbles;
hold a cup to drink from;
stop when spoken to;
show a little cooperation in helping you dress him;
build a tower of two or more blocks and fit a peg into
its proper hole in a board;
have a 5 to 10 word vocabulary.

THE CHILD FROM EIGHTEEN MONTHS TO THREE YEARS

Toddlers

Physical Development ■ Walking brings many changes to the child and everyone around him. From now on life is a compromise between the toddler's fierce desire to be in control and the adult's good sense about what the child's behavior shows he needs. Activities at church must be well planned, for the growing child has many interests, insatiable curiosity and no sense of danger. His environment must be safe for exploring. (See chapter 6 for information on facilities.)

A toddler has a tremendous urge to be independent. He walks, climbs, falls, undresses himself, feeds himself and invades the activities of other children. His growing ability to use his body dominates his attention and energy. No matter how hard he tries, or how earnestly you encourage him, he cannot exercise much deliberate control over his own behavior. He needs space in which to move so he can practice movements which gradually become more relaxed and more controlled. Soft, flexible toys with wheels are excellent for channeling motor activity and cannot hurt the young child.

Physical play, even gentle roughhousing on the floor, is endlessly satisfying to the toddler. He loves to be noisily followed—and caught! He has boundless energy and ideas for play. Playtime helps him develop self-reliance, knowledge of his own powers and confidence in his own abilities. The delightful cooing infant of a year ago has become a bossy, self-oriented toddler in constant motion!

Puzzles, toys such as nesting cans or cups, strings of snap beads, shaped toys which fit over spindles or into containers encourage the child to practice coordinating his muscles and his eyes. A varied selection of toys gives each child the opportunity to play at his present level and to move on to a toy offering more challenge when he is ready. A wise teacher will limit the number of toys available to a child at any one time to avoid overwhelming him with choices.

Emotional Development ■ Basic to a child's welfare is still a strong need to feel loved and accepted by the adults in his life. He must feel love and acceptance even when the things he does are unacceptable. Help him know that you still love him, even when you must redirect his behavior. When he is behaving well, give specific praise as you identify his acceptable actions: "Just look how still Jess stands while I wash his face!"

At each new step in the toddler's development, teachers need to help him learn acceptable behavior. Redirecting him with a toy, conversation or new activity can prevent stubborn resistance. Adults who are consistently firm and friendly, yet understanding of individual differences, help the child begin to control his impulses and develop his own self-control.

The relationship of the child to his teacher is of greater importance than his activities. The toddler who has learned to love and trust the adults in his life is able to confidently explore his surroundings and experience new feelings and new elements in his life. A toddler can build these quality relationships only with adults he sees regularly.

Make it a point to visit the homes of your toddlers. The child loves your interest, and is likely to respond more confidently on Sunday morning. Parents also appreciate a teacher who cares enough to call. Ask the parents for suggestions on activities their child especially enjoys.

The toddler is aware of the emotional states of others and is sensitive to their expressions of anxiety. He has a great desire to be loved and wants to show his affection in return. He imitates the actions and attitudes of significant adults, establishing behavior patterns that will greatly influence his developing personality. For this reason toddlers need teachers who model Christ's love. Criteria for the selection of teachers should be as high for the Toddler Department as for any other group in the Sunday School.

In this seesaw world, the toddler inexpertly pushes to grow faster but then falls back on the love and support of people he trusts. His drive for independence builds on the feelings of safety and love established as an infant. This active trust and sense of security provides a foundation on which the child can begin to think of Jesus as someone who loves and cares for him.

The toddler needs help from adults, even though he often tries to run his life without them. He reaches for door knobs and marches up steps. As an infant he thought his mother was a part of himself—the part that got things done. Now he discovers he can do things himself and this is at the same time exciting and frightening. Bold, independent action is followed by a rush to the familiar security of the teacher or mother. The strong desire for his mother shows that her job of loving and caring for him has been well done. If the child cries when his parents leave, assure the parents that this is because the child loves them, and is a positive sign.

A toddler tests limits as he demands his own way. He often refuses the commands of adults he loves. He is battling for independence and selfhood. Teachers at church and parents at home must decide which things the child can do alone and which have to be restricted for the child's safety. The freedom to explore, test and try things out gives the child the feeling that life is something he can handle. Teachers need to respond to the child by listening attentively, expressing interest in what interests him; by being fair in guiding and correcting the child. When it is necessary to stop a child's play, gently lead him to a new activity. Avoid just saying "No!"

At this age repetition and routine are critical. Retain the same room arrangement. Build on one major concept for at least a month, selecting activities and songs that support that single thrust. Repeat the same basic learning experiences. Also, follow from Sunday to Sunday the same sequence through the morning. The child then feels he can predict what will happen next. This knowledge gives him a satisfying sense of control and security.

The child approaching two continues to push out, finding himself as a separate person. He may now run away from a worker, scream in defiance, or simply decide to cooperate in a most charming and disarming way. No matter how exasperating he may be, the toddler needs love, patience, kindness and firm, gentle control. In addition, he needs time—time to go through this stage, for he cannot bypass it. He is still exploring, deciding and learning what the world is and who he is. He is establishing his independence and a degree of self-determination. Avoid confrontations where possible, or situations which can develop into a battle of wills between you. Rather, give guidance indirectly by the arrangement of your materials and the flow of your activities.

For instance, if a child decides not to help or not come along when you call, continue the activity. The child's curiosity, his desire to be near adults, and his drive to be active will probably pull him into whatever you are doing regardless of his spoken, "no." Try whispering a suggestion to a child. He may whisper back, enchanted with the air of mystery and scarcely able to contain himself until beginning your new idea.

For many children toilet training is a very emotional issue. It is important to deal with "accidents" in a matter-of-fact way. Find out from parents if a child has a particular word to tell he needs to use the toilet. Also be alert to physical signs such as fidgetiness or holding himself. Remember that a young child cannot wait even a few seconds, so be prepared to have a teacher take a child out in the middle of an activity, if necessary.

A toddler nearing his second birthday can begin to recognize some rights of others and make a few choices with other people in mind. When the child feels at ease and happy he will be more cooperative. He needs self-dignity and self-respect in order to have appreciation and esteem for others. With loving guidance and supervision, toddlers can play alongside each other although the desire to share and play with others does not come until later. The young child can begin to help put toys away on storage shelves. He cannot do the job alone. As you help him, take time for a friendly talk giving the child individual attention.

Learning ■ Young children do not wait for formal teaching situations before they learn. One of the nursery teacher's greatest opportunities to help a child is to capitalize on this learning potential. Little ones need to see, touch, smell, hear and taste to learn about their world and the people in it. Nature materials which the child can touch help him accept as real your statements that, "God made this smooth rock...pretty flower, etc." Let children hear a seashell, feel lamb's wool, taste a banana, smell a pine cone and see brightly colored pictures.

Brief conversation about the people and things in a child's world help him build an interest in God. Pictures of familiar objects help the child learn more about things he has experienced. These include pictures of toys, church, plants, animals, and even people. Talk with him about the pictures. Use short, simple sentences. Say, "Here is a bird. God made the bird," as you point to the pictured bird. Frequent conversations which include his name help the toddler grow in his awareness of God and God's love for him. Repetition reinforces these concepts and ideas.

Imaginative play is a powerful learning experience which begins after the child is a year and a half old. He expresses himself, copies gestures and voice inflections, releases anger and frustration, relives experiences which are enjoyable or upsetting. A toddler is attracted to a doll he can hold, cuddle, rock and talk to as the teacher talks with him. A child can express with a doll experiences he has with other people in his life. He can use the doll as an outlet to be a mother, father, brother or sister. When he brings the doll to you, he means, "Let's be friends. Come play with me."

Singing, chanting and impromptu storytelling using the child's name bring wholehearted response from the child. He responds to rhythm and made-up songs about the play activity. You can make up words to a tune the child knows to fit the activity you are doing together. For example, as Miss Edmonds sat looking at a book with three toddlers, she sang to the "Happy Birthday" tune, "I'm so glad Sandy's here, I'm so glad Wendy's here, I'm so glad Erin's here, and I'm glad I'm here, too." The fun you have together is far more important than the quality of your music or composition! The "Farmer in the Dell" and "Mulberry Bush" are also easy tunes to adapt.

Verbal Ability ■ Language gradually becomes more important to the toddler with each passing month. For a while he uses a single word to express a complete thought. "Water," means, "I'm thirsty. I want a drink." As the child begins to talk he improves his ability to retain what is spoken to him. Opportunities for beginning prayer are natural now. There are "pretty flowers," "milk and cookies," "mommy and daddy," "our church" or "my friends" for which to thank God. Brief Bible Thoughts such as, "God cares about you," and "God made everything," may be used very simply in conversation and repeated over and over on a weekly basis. Praying aloud even before the child can talk and join you tells him praying is important to you; and he will want to pray as soon as he is able to talk.

Promotion ■ Prepare toddlers for their promotion into the two-year-old Sunday School department. As a child approaches the time (preferably two years, three months; or two years, six months) when he will move on to an older department, arrange an advance visit, with opportunity to meet one new teacher. Talk with him enthusiastically about what he can do in the new department; that he has now grown big enough to do these things. Encourage his parents to recognize the capabilities of their child and the importance of regular Sunday School attendance in his growing and learning years. Expect many toddlers to be reluctant to move, even reverting to crying when parents bring them to their new room. Patient acceptance of their fears about this change will keep any upsets to a minimum.

Two-Year-Olds

Physical Development ■ The two-year-old's body demands exercise. He's constantly on the move—running, jumping, and climbing. Because the large muscles in his legs and arms are developing, he is often not sure of his balance. He tumbles often. Plan for open spaces in your room in which the child is free to move. Keep furnishings at a minimum. Provide equipment such as a rocking boat and climbing steps that allow him to use his large muscles. Use simple finger fun and activity songs that allow him to reach and stretch, to jump and clap.

The two-year-old's small hand and finger muscles are not developed enough to allow sophisticated manipulation. For art activities, provide large sheets of blank paper and jumbo crayons or long-handled paint brushes. (Do NOT expect a child under six to color within an outline!) Provide puzzles with a few large pieces; have large spools or beads to string. Provide large blocks or cartons he can stack and manipulate.

The two-year-old tires easily. His constant activity is a source of real fatigue which is often the cause of unacceptable behavior. He does not know how to stop and rest, so provide alternating times of active and quiet play. Be alert to the child who needs to "slow down." Gently redirect his attention to looking at a book or working a puzzle with you.

For example, Mrs. Cook watched as Nancy prepared to feed her doll at the Home Living area. She knew Nancy had been very active all morning and she noticed that Nancy was beginning to hit children who came too near.

Mrs. Cook said, "Nancy, your baby has had a good lunch. I think she'd like to hear a story. I have a new book she will like." Gently she took Nancy and her doll in her lap and together they looked at a picture book. As they sat quietly talking about the pictures, Nancy began to relax and was soon able to rejoin the other children.

Mental and Emotional Development ■ The two-year-old is an explorer rather than a creator. Because he learns through his senses, he curiously pokes, feels, hits, tastes, listens to and smells the world about him. Peter was watching the fish at the

God's Wonders table. Suddenly, water was splashing everywhere as Peter's hand went into the water and after the fish. Mr. Clark gently removed Peter's hand from the bowl. As he dried Peter and the tabletop, he said, "Our goldfish are for us to look at, not for us to touch. Watch the fish's tail move as he swims." As they watched together, Mr. Clark sang, "Who made the goldfish? God did..." Mr. Clark knew Peter was not being "bad." He was simply attempting to satisfy his curiosity about the fish.

The two-year-old's interest span is short. Expect him to pick up a toy, drop it and move on to something else. He is likely to participate briefly in one activity and then move to another. Two children may play side by side, but each will be involved in his own activity, with little interaction. Provide a variety of activities of interest to twos and do not expect a child to remain interested in any one thing for more than a few minutes.

The two-year-old sometimes says, "No," when he means, "Yes." Because he is on the move and is curious about everything, the word a two-year-old hears most frequently is No! He often uses the word himself because of its simplicity and familiarity. Phrase your suggestions in the form of statements, rather than questions. Avoid, "Do you want to...?" Rather say, "Please bring the book to me...Thank you, Tom."

The two-year-old likes to do things for himself. His frequent plea is "let me do it!" Offer assistance only as needed. However, during an activity be alert for any child who might be reaching the point of frustration: step in with a suggestion to help him succeed. "Jan, your puzzle has a pretty flower in it. I wonder if this piece will fit here." Then praise the child's successful attempts. Provide materials and equipment he can easily manage.

The two-year-old's vocabulary is increasing. However, he uses more words than he understands, so he doesn't always mean what he says! When talking with the two-year-old use simple words and short sentences. Avoid symbolism! Speak slowly and clearly, without "talking down" to the child. He enjoys listening to songs, finger fun and rhythms; he likes to hear his favorites over and over again. Expect a two-year-old's initial response to be one of observation rather than participation.

The two-year-old is still becoming aware of himself as a person. Everything he does relates to himself. Sing songs that include his name, such as, "Who made Danny? God did..." Use his name often in your conversation. When he talks to you, look into his face and give him your undivided attention. Let him feel that, at least for that moment, he is the most important person in the room to you. Plan activities and provide equipment whereby he can experience success. Offer words of praise and encouragement as you refer to his specific actions.

The two-year-old has little sense of time. He can't be hurried. Do not expect an immediate response to your requests. Allow plenty of time for moving from one part of the schedule to the next; for putting on coats, for wash-up and toilet details.

Social Development ■ The two-year-old has little regard for the rights of others. At times it seems as if *no* and *mine* are the only words he knows! Sharing and taking turns are new words and new ideas to most twos. When disputes occur, a two will more likely respond to distraction than to reasoning. "Chris, that's Eric's truck. Here is a red truck for you to use." Provide duplicates of favorite toys.

The two-year-old seeks close physical contact with loving understanding adults. Jesus called little children to Him and rebuked those who would send them away. We can easily imagine that He held them on His lap and listened patiently to their chatter. Those who guide twos need to be kind, patient Christians who love little children and who are willing to give the kind of attention the child's behavior shows he needs. A smile and a friendly pat might meet the needs of one child while a hug or a few moments of cuddling might be the answer for another. An effective teacher knows the needs of the children and is able to respond to these needs.

The two-year-old's moments of fear, disappointment and frustration require the help of an understanding adult. Should a child cry when his mother leaves, avoid shaming him. Help him feel secure by giving him personal attention, such as holding him on your lap as you look at a book. Ask his mother to leave something, such as gloves or a scarf to help assure the child she will return.

The two-year-old comes to you on Sunday morning with the potential to learn many things. If you prepare your room and thoughts ahead of time, he will learn and grow in wisdom and stature and favor with God and Man.

Milestones of Development

The ability to talk is the dominant advance made by the child between 18 months and three years. The child is changing rapidly during this period, and is characterized by a bountiful and boundless energy that adults often wish they could harness. The child is a demanding runabout who requires all of the stamina, creativity and patience the learning leader has to give.

By two years old the toddler may:
be walking and climbing on chairs and stairs, always on the go!
scribble on paper spontaneously and vigorously (the wall, too, if you're not careful), and imitate your strokes with crayon;
use words in one- and two-word sentences;
point to his nose, eyes, hair, ears when asked to identify them;
build a high tower with blocks;
fill a container with smaller objects;
feed himself at snack times;
turn pages of book to look at pictures;
throw a ball into a box.

Between the ages of two and three years the toddler may:
run and play with great energy;

tire easily, becoming fussy and irritable;
say many words and make sentences of several words;
understand most normal conversation;
be interested in everything in the world about him;
play happily by himself, with occasional
interaction with others;
be bowel-trained and have daytime bladder control;
know where objects belong and can help to put them away;
follow one direction at a time.

THE CHILD FROM THREE TO FIVE YEARS

God has entrusted you with the responsibility and opportunity of helping young children learn some vital and basic Bible truths. To help a child learn effectively, those who guide him must be aware of his pattern of growth. Each child is an individual and develops at his own rate. His rate of growth is determined by many factors, including health and environment. However, there is enough similarity among children of the same age that common characteristics can be noted. These characteristics should be used as a guide when planning learning activities for the child; they should never be used as a mold in which to place every child when he reaches his third or fourth birthday.

Three-Year-Olds

When a three-year-old comes to church he brings all of himself. He brings a total child who grows in his own way and at his own rate. He needs a wide variety of experiences to help him keep growing as God planned.

Physical Development ■ The three-year-old is developing effective large muscle control. He is sure on his feet, with an accurate sense of his limits. He enjoys activities and materials, such as blocks for building, that encourage the use of his large muscles. The child needs room in which to move about, so keep furnishings to a minimum. Provide a choice of activities and freedom to move from one activity to another.

The three-year-old's control of small finger and hand muscles is not yet fully developed. He cannot cut accurately with scissors or color within an outline. He is ready to experiment with paste; collages are a great activity for him. He needs beads to string and puzzles to solve. Give him pegs and pegboards and a wide variety of utensils to use with clay. Repeat familiar activities often as they support learning aims.

Three-year-olds play hard and tire easily. Provide a balance of active and quiet play. Be alert to the child who is becoming overstimulated. Guide him to a quiet activity, such as working a puzzle or looking at a picture book with you. During the second hour of your morning schedule, plan for a rest time of not less than 10 minutes. Include a light snack, also.

Mental and Emotional Development ▪ Imaginative play begins to flower during this year. Simple imitation of an adult example gradually develops into extended efforts to be "Mommy," "Daddy," "Fireman" or "Teacher." There is little true interaction in this play, and several "mommies" are likely to occupy the Home Living center at one time. However, the child's ability to think of himself as someone else is an important step forward in mental growth.

The three-year-old participates only as long as he is interested. A variety of activities is necessary to meet constantly changing levels of attention. As Mrs. Graham told a story of ways God planned for food to grow, she noticed that some children were becoming restless. Without stopping her story, she said, "And God planned for apples to grow on trees. Let's pretend we are apple trees and stretch our branches way up into the sky....Let's pretend the wind is blowing our branches...." As the children moved their arms high overhead, she sang, "The apple trees are swaying..." When the song ended and everyone sat down again, she showed a food picture and continued her story by saying, "Look what else God made that's good to eat!"

Mrs. Graham recognized two needs: (1) the children's need to stretch and move, and (2) her need to regain the children's attention. Both needs were met by giving the children an opportunity to sing and move. They were actively participating in the story. The second need was met by immediately drawing the children's attention to the picture.

Children also listen better when they have first had an opportunity to share their ideas. Then, require them to wait as you take your turn. Keep your turn brief, however. A good rule of thumb for story length with young children is one minute for each year of age.

A three-year-old does not understand symbolism! Use simple stories told in literal terms—words that mean exactly what they say.

He also may have difficulty understanding directions. Give one brief direction at a time. Allow a child to complete the task before suggesting the next one. Rather than saying, "Pick up the toys, then go sit down," say, "It's time to put the toys on this shelf." Work with the children, commending them for their efforts. As they finish, say, "Thank you for putting every toy in just the right place. Now it's time to sit on the rug and sing some songs." The leader should begin some activity songs while children are gathering. The music will draw the more reticent and occupy those who have cooperated immediately.

Social Development ■ The three-year-old is sensitive to your actions, attitudes and feelings. It is important for you to know each child as an individual. Jesus was keenly aware of people as individuals. For instance, when He was surrounded by those who had come to see Him, He stopped and called Zaccheus— by name! You represent that highly personal love of God to the young child.

As Sam and his family rode home from church, Sam announced, "God didn't come to Sunday School today." After a moment of silence, he added, "But He sent my teacher." To the young child you are God's representative. Help the child to know God made him and that God loves him, by loving him yourself. Help him to know Jesus as a kind, loving friend, by being a good listener.

Use the child's name often as you talk with him. Listen attentively to what he tells you. Scott was trying earnestly to tell his teacher something he considered of great importance. His teacher kept on preparing materials for another part of the morning schedule, occasionally offering a noncommittal "uh-huh." Finally, in desperation Scott said, "Listen to me!"

"I am listening," his teacher replied.

"But you are not listening with your face!" was Scott's comment.

Scott in his three-year-old way distinguished between having someone merely hear his words and someone listen to him attentively. When you talk with a child, sit or bend down so you are at his eye level, give him your undivided attention (stop what you are doing), respond to his words appropriately by sharing his enthusiasm or offering a bit of sympathy. As you show genuine interest in each child, you are demonstrating God's love in a way the child can understand. The Lord Jesus' command that we love one another becomes alive with meaning. God's Word demonstrated is more convincing to young children than God's Word explained.

The three-year-old still likes to play alone but also enjoys being with other children. While he has not left his self-centered "me, my and mine" world, he frequently engages in parallel play, often advancing into real interaction and cooperation. Offer activities that allow him to participate successfully alongside other children, with opportunities available for interaction.

Three-year-olds often lack the language to begin a conversation. Instead they say, "Hi, play with me," by bumping the other child or grabbing his toys. Create opportunities that foster healthy social development. For instance. "Terry, you really have lots of pegs. I think John needs some more pegs. What can you do to help John?... You are a kind friend to share pegs with John."

Provide activities that encourage children to relate to one another. Identify and interpret specific acts of kindness so a child knows what to do to be loving and friendly. Be ready with words of praise and encouragement when a child exhibits acceptable behavior toward another child.

Sharing and taking turns are still hard for most three-year-olds. Identify what these words mean. "First I roll the ball to Mary. Mary rolls it back to me. Now I roll it to Sue. We're taking turns!" A concerned teacher will be sure that each child gets his or her turn so he or she will not conclude that taking turns means losing out!

Before a child can relate satisfactorily to others, he needs to feel good about himself. Help him develop self-confidence and a healthy self-image by providing experiences in which each child can succeed, being careful to introduce activities that will challenge rapidly developing abilities. Alan had successfully put together every puzzle in the rack several times in recent weeks. Miss Payne commented on his achievement as she brought out two new puzzles, each with several more pieces than the others. The new challenge restimulated Alan's interest in doing puzzles. More important, Alan learned another lesson that built his confidence—and his thankfulness to God for "giving Alan hands and eyes to do puzzles."

Four-Year-Olds

The four-year-old is much advanced in abilities but very similar in needs to a three-year-old. Both age groups need to explore new materials but their use of them varies greatly depending on the individual level of skill development.

Physical Development ■ The four-year-old is in a period of rapid physical growth. His coordination rapidly improves and he is stronger and more confident than he was at three. He still seems to be constantly on the go—running, jumping, walking or climbing, needing open spaces so he can move about freely.

Freehand, creative art activities are the most satisfying. Continue to provide large sheets of paper and large crayons. (Do not expect a four-year-old to color within lines!) Some four-year-olds may begin to draw pictures as such, a face, a flower, a house. At the paint easel he uses his large brush to make sweeping strokes of bright color.

Because the four-year-old is gaining in his control of the small muscles, he enjoys attempting activities that involve fine coordination. Provide opportunities for him to button, zip a zipper, lace shoes and cut on a heavy line. Make them fun by letting the child practice and not drawing attention to performance, but rather to perseverance.

Like the three-year-old, the four-year-old tires quickly. His rapid growth and constant activity cause him to become easily fatigued. His tiredness may result in unacceptable behavior. Alternate times of active and quiet play throughout your morning schedule.

Mental and Emotional Development ■ The four-year-old has a strong desire to learn reasons for everything he sees. He is curious and questioning. His favorite words seem to be *how, what* and *why.* He enjoys experimenting with words. Making up silly-sounding rhymes is great fun and gives good practice in improving language skills. While questions are common, he continues most learning in much the same way as when he was three—by doing. Continue to provide materials for children to touch, smell, see and even taste. Use everyday objects and activities to relate Scripture truths to the child's life. Use simple words and literal phrases that mean exactly what they say.

The four-year-old can now concentrate for longer periods of

time than when he was three. However, his attention span is still short. He is easily distracted and his rapidly developing large muscles make it difficult for him to sit still for more than four or five minutes. Provide a variety of activities and materials, selecting those most appropriate to specific learning aims. For example, one Sunday the Table Activity may be puzzles. The next Sunday it could be a matching game. Make changes from one hour to the next, also. During Sunday School the Home Living center may be involved in doll play, then during Church Time, a food preparation activity could be used. Rotation of activities saves money, wear and tear on supplies, and adds variety. Never change everything at once. One or two different activities is adequate. This retains the flavor of the room while simultaneously adding interest.

The four-year-old has advanced considerably in one year in his ability to participate with other children in group activities. Because of his limited attention span, the activities should be kept brief. He enjoys group singing, prayer and conversation about activities just finished. Use large teaching pictures to reinforce basic concepts.

The four-year-old is often testing his world. He may exhibit unacceptable behavior just to see how far he can go. He finds security in the very limits he defies; yet he needs the security of limits that do not hinder his freedom to experiment. Be consistent in your every-Sunday guidance. Be positive in your suggestions. Emphasize the behavior you desire rather than the kind you want to discourage. Say, "We keep the blocks in the block area" rather than "Don't bring the blocks to the home corner!" The word "don't" often makes a child want to resist.

Many fours can write at least part of their first name. They will want to do as much of it as they can, and will watch intensely whenever you write it for them. Print their name clearly, using a capital followed by lower case letters. If a child is interested, form a dot pattern which the child can trace to practice making his name.

The four-year-old may exaggerate his abilities. He brags and boasts about himself. "I can climb to the very top of this building; I can run and jump better than anyone else!" Do not dispute his claims, but redirect his conversation. "You can run and jump because your legs are growing strong, just as God planned. I need a strong boy like you to help put these blocks away."

Social Development ■ The four-year-old longs for and actively seeks adult approval. He responds to friendliness and wants to be loved, especially by his teacher. Be interested in what interests him and in what he has to say. Be ready with a friendly greeting that recognizes him as an individual: "That's a pretty orange shirt you're wearing, Kevin. Is it new?...I like the stripes." Give him opportunities to lead with your support. Let him serve a snack, or hold a picture. This will build confidence in his own ability.

The four-year-old shows a growing interest in doing things with other children. While younger fours may still prefer to work alone or in parallel play, older fours prefer to work in small groups of two or three children.

The four-year-old likes to pretend. "I'm the daddy and you're the mother" kinds of play occur frequently in the Home Living area as children now begin to interact in taking simple family roles. Children also like to play out experiences. "We're going to the park today. Everybody get ready," a four is likely to announce. Provide both male and female clothing and accessories for dress-up.

Milestones of Development

To a child between three and four years old, everything is a beautiful, fascinating mystery just waiting to be solved. The child is full of whys, mischievousness, imagination and willingness, all waiting to be challenged.

Between three and four years old the child may:
unbutton and button large side and front buttons;
unlace and take off his shoes;
put on his shoes if someone holds the tongues down;
put on and take off galoshes, if they're large enough to slip
easily over his shoes;
build actual structures with blocks;
begin to draw and paint simple pictures of objects and people;
begin to use numbers to count objects;
learn nursery rhymes, songs and finger fun;
use scissors to cut on heavy, straight lines;
interact with others in imaginative play;
recognize his name in print;
and write at least part of it;
identify primary colors by name;
take care of his own toilet needs.

THE CHILD FROM FIVE TO SIX

While a large number of three- and four-year-olds attend day-care centers and nursery schools, in many regions most, if not all, fives attend kindergarten. The child who experiences regular group experiences will tend to have advantages in terms of interaction with other children, ability to participate in a group, and skill in using common learning materials. However, the basic developmental sequence will remain the same.

Physical Development

The five-year-old is still physically active. His strength, agility and balance are well coordinated, and develop at an equal rate. He needs opportunities for movement of his body, arms and legs. Dramatic play, finger fun and activity songs encourage jumping, stretching and bending. Block building is an excellent every-Sunday learning activity. Fives need plenty of room in which to move about, so keep furnishings in the room to a minimum.

Freehand drawing and painting with large crayons or brushes is still most appropriate. Also provide clay or salt/flour dough for the children to use. Alternate active and quiet experiences so children are not required to sit still for more than four or five minutes.

While the child's growth rate is slowing, girls are maturing more rapidly than boys in their physical development. Expect boys to become restless sooner during a large group activity.

The five-year-old's small muscles are under better control than when he was four. He enjoys more sophisticated toys; however, do not expect him to color accurately within lines. Also, cutting accurately is still difficult for fives, although they can follow a simple, curved line.

Mental and Emotional Development

The five-year-old likes to help, and thrives on the approval and attention he receives. Helping tasks such as bringing materials from the art shelf or carrying scraps to the wastebasket also help the child work off some of his excess energy. Give him responsibilities which he can perform successfully. Praise him when he completes a task.

As children were finishing making cookies at the Home Living table, Mr. Walters said, "Nathan, the table is sticky. What do you think we should do?"

"Wash it off," Nathan replied.

"Good thinking, Nathan. Can you find a wet sponge to use?" Nathan looked around and spotted a sponge next to the dishpan of water Mr. Walters had brought to the room. He quickly dipped the sponge in the water and thoroughly scrubbed the table.

"Nathan, you know where to find the sponge, and you know how to clean the table. You have learned to use your mind and your arms to be a helper like the Bible says. Can you remember what the Bible says about being helpers?"

" 'With love, help one another,' " Nathan responded. He had

heard Mr. Walters use that verse several times as they were making cookies. Not only could he repeat it, he could demonstrate it!

Five-year-olds may stay with some activities longer than younger children. One Sunday Shelly spent the total Bible Learning Activity Time in the Home Living corner, caring for dolls and setting the table. The next week, however, she started at the painting easel, moved to the book shelf, looked through the magnifying glass in God's Wonders, then returned to the book shelf. Choices of activities provide for these variations in each child's interests.

When you tell a story, eye contact with each child is the key to sustaining interest. Each child needs to feel you are talking directly to him. Use action words such as *run, walk* or *climb*. Change the inflection of your voice to create feelings of excitement, weariness, happiness, etc. Occasionally whisper to create a quiet mood. "The wind howled. The big waves crashed against the little boat. Then, Jesus said, 'Be still.' The wind stopped howling; the waves stopped crashing (whisper) and everything was calm and still."

Most five-year-olds are learning to write (print) in public school kindergarten. Be aware of each child's level of accomplishment. Be careful to praise each child for what he can do and not compare him to others.

It is a beautiful experience to watch the face of a child as he pours his whole being into printing his name. He bites his tongue, squints one eye, and tilts his head to the side as he attempts to form the letters which are *his name*. Then, as the last letter is finished, he breathes deeply and smiles contentedly.

His name is usually the child's first written word. It is filled with great emotional meaning for the child and the way he first learns to print it is the way he will want to continue printing it.

Be sure to use a capital followed by *lower case* letters.

Kindergarten is an introduction into the academic world of numbers, letters and a few simple words. Activities that contribute directly to beginning reading skills include: blocks, puzzles and matching games, all of which help a child's awareness of shape and size relationships. Books are also important in building interest in reading. Art activities can be enriched by letting the child dictate comments about the "picture" which the teacher can attach to the paper. Also, make word cards and tape them to objects around the room. Use words like, Bible, Gifts, Picture, Blocks, Window, Coats, etc. Refer to them from time to time and the children will begin to "read" them.

The five-year-old is curious and eager to learn. He learns rapidly and asks many questions. Answer his questions simply in ways that will stimulate his own thinking. Avoid telling a child what he can find out for himself. Bobby was using the magnet at the God's Wonders table. "Why won't the magnet pick up this box?" he asked.

"Let's see if we can find out," answered Mrs. Collins. "Will it pick up this nail?" Together, Mrs. Collins and Bobby tried to pick up various objects with the magnet. As they worked, Mrs. Collins stimulated Bobby's thinking until he reached the conclusion that a magnet only picks up certain kinds of metal.

A five-year-old still relies on his senses for most of his learning. Use objects he can see, touch, smell, taste and hear. Provide many opportunities for activities which are within his ability. Be sensitive enough to step in when help is needed, but not to interfere when the child is able to complete a task successfully.

The five-year-old still interprets words literally; he does not understand symbolic concepts. Use words that mean exactly what they say. Instead of singing a symbolic song, such as, "The B-I-B-L-E," sing "Our Bible":
"Our Bible tells how God loves us,
God loves us,
God loves us.
Our Bible tells how God loves us,
how God loves you and me."
The five-year-old still needs affection and security. He may

appear sometimes to be strong and confident. But he is still easily upset and needs dependable adult support. He can go quickly from bravado to tears. He can also go quickly from tears to laughter. This does not mean the feelings are shallow. It means the five-year-old is still a child of the immediate present. Past and future have little hold on his attention. He cares about the current moment, the people and things he can see right now.

Social Development

The child needs attention from other children and adults. He is anxious for adult approval and wants to establish a good relationship between himself and his teacher. Stacy thought she had found a way to win approval by tattling. Her teacher wisely just said, "I know you want children to do right things. You do what is right so the others can watch you and copy you."

Give the child individual attention before any negative behavior occurs. Initiate conversations, listen closely when he talks to you. Give a smile, a hug or a pat on the shoulder to show he is special to you. This will reduce the need for negative attention-getting.

The five-year-old enjoys working in small groups with much real cooperation occurring. However, when more than two or three children participate in an activity, adult help is needed to insure that every child can be involved. Even when only two or three play together, adult help is often needed to suggest ideas that will keep the activity moving.

One Sunday, Mr. Gomez planned an activity to encourage thankfulness for food. He posted on the bulletin board a long sheet of butcher paper, divided into three sections: Breakfast, Lunch, Dinner. He provided food pictures torn from magazines, scissors to trim the pictures, and paste. The children selected pictures of food they were thankful for, and that would be appropriate for specific meals. There was considerable conversation among the children as they decided whether certain pictures went better under "breakfast" or "lunch." As they worked, Mr.

Gomez commented that God made our food. He expressed his own thanks to God for it, and gave opportunity for the children to do so also.

The children in your department come from different and varied backgrounds. There will be children from Christian homes where the love of God is a natural part of everyday conversation. There will be children who have never heard about God's love. There will be children who have been in Sunday School since birth and there will be those who are attending for the first time. Meet each child where he is; plan experiences through which he can learn of God's love. "Teach a child to choose the right path, and when he is older he will remain upon it" (Prov. 22:6, *TLB*).

Milestones of Development

Between the ages of five and six, the child may:
tie his own shoelaces, though not usually tight enough to stay;
participate in extended cooperative play with
one or two friends;
write his name clearly without help;
read some simple words;
cut with scissors along a curved line;
draw or paint easily recognizable pictures of people and objects;
recognize tints and shades of common colors;
recall short Bible verses he has heard frequently;
talk accurately about recent events;
pronounce most common words correctly.

FOOTNOTE

1. *Little Ones Sing*, revised edition, (Glendale, Calif.: G/L Publications, 1972) p. 143.

Learning to Develop Leaders

Helper.
Worker.
Attendant.
Baby-sitter.
Churches have used all kinds of terms to describe the people who work with young children. However, there is one word that accurately describes anyone who is personally involved with little ones:
Teacher.
Children are always learning. And they are always learning from the people who talk with and care for them.
Whether this learning is positive or negative depends on what the teacher does with the child. And what the teacher does often depends on the support the teacher receives from leaders.
The following section describes the duties of the people who work with young children on Sunday morning at church. Each person performs an essential part in building a strong, effective ministry.

WHO ARE THE LEADERS AND WHAT DO THEY DO?

Teacher

Early Childhood teachers are:
Creators of an environment and atmosphere in which children can learn;
sources of love;
models for children to emulate;
guides in learning experiences.

Teachers of two-year-olds through five-year-olds are responsible to:

1. Prepare and guide one Bible learning activity for each session.

2. Prepare and present the Bible story each week to his own class, and guide children in completing their activity page.

3. Participate in large group activities and transitions between activities.

Teachers of babies and toddlers should:

1. Prepare interaction activities appropriate to children's development and unit learning aims, creating a safe, interesting environment.

2. Focus primary attention for care and interaction on a small group of children as assigned by leader.

3. Assist with other children as necessary.

All Sunday School teachers should:

4. Maintain home contact with his own class members and families.

5. Seek to win unchurched families to Christ and the church.

6. Attend and participate in regular departmental planning meetings.

7. Take advantage of training opportunities to improve his teaching.

The Teacher's Morning ■ Teachers arrive on Sunday morning in time to set up activity areas before the first child arrives. This usually means arriving at least 20 minutes before the time Sunday School is scheduled to begin. As children arrive, they immediately choose a Bible learning activity. The teacher at each activity guides the children in learning experiences related to the lesson's Bible teaching/learning aim. Baby and toddler teachers move among the activities, caring primarily for the children assigned to them. Each teacher's responsibility is determined at the regular department planning meeting.

Following these Bible learning activities, teachers of twos

through fives guide children in putting away materials, then moving together for group singing and sharing. The teachers sit among the children as the Department Leader directs the group. Group experiences with toddlers often occur spontaneously, as when one teacher sings a song and the children come over to investigate.

Because children need to find security in a close relationship with one adult, each teacher of twos through fives is assigned a small Bible story class. The teacher tells the Bible story to his own class group each Sunday. This continuing relationship with a teacher helps a child feel loved and special.

After the Bible story, the Bible teaching/learning objective is reinforced by an activity page used in the small class groups. The teacher shows a completed page, talks about the truth it illustrates, then guides children in completing their own page. Thus each child has an opportunity to respond to the truth that was emphasized in the Bible story.

Teachers continue with the children until the Church Time staff is ready to assume leadership.

The Teacher's Week ■ *Preparation:* Teaching young children involves more than simply walking in the door. Thoughtful planning is necessary to make sure the activities provided produce positive learning. Each teacher needs to spend time each week in study of the Bible passage and the curriculum materials. Without this planning, the teacher's effectiveness will diminish and many learning opportunities will be lost.

No teacher works alone. Each is a part of the whole ministry of the church and Sunday School. Regular meetings to plan, pray and share are vitally necessary to all teachers. These planning meetings are not only a privilege, but a responsibility.

Parents: Children are in an Early Childhood department for only an hour or two each week. They spend the major share of their time at home. True concern for the child's spiritual life, therefore, compels a teacher to cultivate a relationship with the parents, sharing with them the objectives of the department and insights into their child's spiritual growth. Evidence that someone cares about their child will draw many parents closer to the church and to God. Noticing absences and remembering birthdays, plus visits to the home each quarter with curriculum materials, shows parents and children the teacher really cares. A bridge of mutual trust and understanding between church and home is built in this manner, opening doors for teachers to share the reality of Christian faith.

Sensitive teachers will be aware of homes in the neighborhood in which there are small children who do not attend Sunday School. Personal contacts that show a loving concern for these children may result in parents bringing these children to Sunday School. Such contacts have resulted in entire families being won to Christ.

Department Leader

Each *Department Leader* works within a department guiding both teachers and children. The leader should have experiences as a teacher in order to provide both instruction and example in fulfilling these duties:

1. Coordinate and evaluate all activities within the department.
2. Lead the large group activities of the department.
3. Insure that each child receives a personal greeting at the door.
4. Suggest prospective new staff for the department.
5. Maintain proper teacher-pupil ratios.
6. Lead teachers in building relationships with families, seeking to win those who are unsaved.
7. Recommend space, equipment and material needs of the department.
8. Communicate necessary information among the staff.
9. Organize and lead regular department planning meetings.
10. Communicate regularly with Church Time staff to coordinate the Church Time and Sunday School plans.

Supporting the Team ■ The Department Leader should be alert to the way the entire Sunday morning program is being conducted. Compliments for jobs well done will give teachers a sense of satisfaction in their work. Constructive suggestions, tactfully given, will always be appreciated by concerned teachers. Leaders need to encourage teachers to try new, well-planned techniques that will help them achieve a greater measure of success. Leaders also need to listen attentively to teachers' suggestions and complaints; then make an attempt to incorporate any constructive ideas.

Guiding Bible Learning Activities ■ The Department Leader needs to be free to greet children when they first arrive. The first moments a child is in the room set the tone for the rest of the child's morning. Greet each child by name, bending or squatting to his eye level. Assist as necessary in hanging up his coat or sweater, and putting on his name tag.

Invite the child to the Love Gift center, then help him choose a Bible learning activity. "Which would you like to do first?" is a good question to ask. If the child is shy or crying, looking at a book while sitting on a teacher's lap is often effective in providing needed security.

As teachers and children work on Bible learning activities, the leader should be available to deal with any problems that arise. Typical situations needing the leader's help include: a child reluctant to participate; a crying child; too many children in one area; a behavior problem. As the leader meets these needs there are many opportunities to talk informally with both children and teachers, setting a positive, friendly tone for the whole room. The leader is thus able to observe teacher's strengths and weaknesses without being threatening to the teacher.

Organizing Together Time ■ The Department Leader gives the signal when it is time to move to the large group. He begins an activity song or finger fun as the first children arrive at the circle.

This frees the teachers to assist slower children in finishing cleanup before all join the large group. Since the leader has been moving among the small groups he can easily relate songs and other features to the activities children have just completed.

From week to week, one or other of the teachers may assist in some aspect of the large group time. A team effort will enrich this time for the children, and help teachers improve their capabilities.

Supporting Bible Story Time ■ After Together Time, teachers meet with their small groups to tell the Bible story. The leader again is available to assist as needed, especially when a restless child needs a calming hand on the shoulder or a whisper in the ear. In some cases it is necessary to remove a child. The leader can look at books with him, insuring that the child is still allowed to learn.

The Department Leader also directs teachers in providing a smooth transition into Church Time.

Filling Personnel Needs ■ The Department Leader is closely aware of the department's personnel requirements and should be involved in seeking additional staff when the need arises. He should work closely with the Division Coordinator or General Superintendent in order to maintain a proper teacher/pupil ratio within the department. Through the course of the year a department's attendance may change enough to warrant adding teachers or even starting a new department. Leaders should be alert to this situation so proper action can be taken in time to maintain a good quality program.

Evaluate Facilities ■ The leader can recommend and implement many improvements within the department by working with the teachers to help them upgrade teaching techniques, materials and equipment. One of the most common areas requiring continuous evaluation and improvement is that of inadequate facilities, which can rarely be corrected quickly or simply. A leader who knows what is needed and why it is needed can make solid and realistic recommendations for improvement within the scope of the church's situation. Continuing discussions by the leader with the staff of the Sunday School often produce satisfactory improvements for all divisions.

Reaching Homes ▪ Good communication between teachers and parents is essential in order to build both home and church into an effective teaching partnership. The Department Leader must take initiative in getting parents and teachers together. Invite the parents to come and observe your program. This will help the children adjust and also build a bond with the families. Also, to lead the department effectively in becoming a potent force in evangelism, the leader should set an example in contacting and visiting homes.

The leader should also seek to develop a good working relationship with the young adult classes attended by children's parents. As new families bring their children to an Early Childhood department, the leader needs to alert the appropriate adult class to these potential new members.

Regular Planning Meetings ▪ Much of the success of an Early Childhood department, regardless of size, depends on good relationships among its staff. The Department Leader needs to meet regularly with the entire department staff for prayer, evaluation and planning. Many departments meet once a week to get ready for the next Sunday. Meeting once at the beginning of every unit is the minimum necessary to produce consistent improvement. A unit planning meeting saves time by allowing the staff to survey four or five lessons at one time.

The Department Leader should also talk individually with teachers between meetings. This keeps the department operating smoothly, and provides opportunity for the leader to share insights gained from observation during the Sunday sessions.

**A UNIT PLANNING MEETING
FOR AN EARLY CHILDHOOD DEPARTMENT**

7:00 *Ministry to Each Other*
   ■ Study of Bible passage to be taught to children
   ■ Sharing of personal victories and challenges
   ■ Prayer for each other's needs

7:30 *Teacher Improvement Feature*
   ■ Focus on one skill each month (music, storytelling, discipline, creative art, blocks, etc.)
   ■ Evaluate previous unit in light of this skill

8:00 *Preview New Unit*
   ■ Teaching/Learning Aims
   ■ Bible coverage—Main thrust of stories
   ■ Bible verses
   ■ Music to support aims
   ■ Bible learning activity assignments

8:30 *Plan First Lesson of Unit*
   ■ Lesson Aims
   ■ Bible learning activity materials and conversation
   ■ Bible story ideas and resources
   ■ Activity page

9:00 *Dismiss*

General Superintendent/Division Coordinator

The *General Superintendent* is responsible to the church for the work of the Sunday School. He must work closely with every Department Leader.

A *Division Coordinator* should be appointed when a church has three or more Early Childhood departments. This leader is responsible to the General Superintendent and assumes direction for all functions in this division. The coordinator then

THE EARLY CHILDHOOD DIVISION

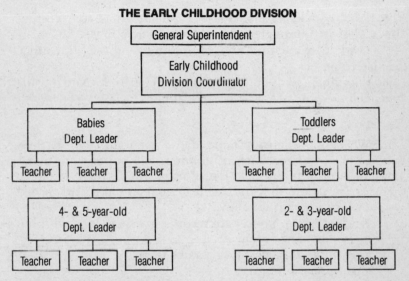

works closely with the department leaders, guiding by suggestion and demonstration to make the teaching/learning in these departments more effective.

Both the General Superintendent and Division Coordinator must be knowledgeable in Early Childhood education in order to guide other people in their work. The main leadership tasks include responsibility to:

1. Lead the division (made up of all the Early Childhood departments) in planning, conducting and evaluating its work.

2. Communicate to the division the goals of the church in areas such as: curriculum, outreach, teacher standards, relationships with parents, etc.

3. Lead teachers in setting goals for improvement and in evaluating progress toward these goals.

4. Work with department leaders in enlisting and training new staff in accordance with church policy.

5. Guide leaders of Sunday School and church time in providing a coordinated total morning program.

6. Work with department leaders to insure in-service training for current staff through regular planning meetings.

7. Lead in evaluating and improving facilities and other needed resources.

8. Coordinate with other church agencies to develop a well-balanced program of Christian education.

Secretary

Sunday School efficiency depends on accurate records. Secretaries need to keep track of children and supplies to make possible an orderly and effective ministry. The secretary should:

1. Arrive before the first child to sign in child and record parent's location during morning.

2. Keep accurate, up-to-date records in accordance with the system used by the church.

3. Care for and use children's name tags.

4. Take care of love-gift money.

5. Order supplies for the department.

6. Prepare activity sheets for Bible Story groups. (Many secretaries secure help on this from senior citizen's groups.)

7. Attend planning meetings to record plans, determine supply needs and share attendance information with teachers.

8. Send cards to absent children.

CHURCH TIME STAFF

Church Time is a vital part of the Sunday School's ministry to young children. By providing a second hour program following Sunday School, a department doubles its time for accomplishing its teaching/learning objectives. The most effective use of this valuable time for young children is to continue the same procedures that were used during the first hour, reinforcing the same Bible learning. Young children need repetition more than they need a total change of pace. Here are three patterns churches have found successful for staffing this important program. In each case, Church Time personnel need the same curriculum resources as provided for Sunday School teachers in order to build on what occurred the first hour.

A Separate, Permanent Staff

Some churches use an entirely new staff for the second hour. The Church Time staff serves on the same regular basis as the Sunday School teachers. Both staffs meet together for planning. The Church Time Leader works closely with the Sunday School Department Leader following the direction established in the first hour. Separate staffs work well in churches that have more than one morning worship service.

Sunday School Continuity/Rotating Volunteers

The second plan has been used in many churches to insure a smooth carry-over between the two hours. One Sunday School teacher teaches in both Sunday School and Church Time for one month. The other teachers are replaced during Church Time by volunteers who will also serve the full month. The Sunday School teacher serves as leader of the second hour staff. The next month another teacher and a new group of volunteers take over.

By having the same teacher and volunteers together for the full month, the unit objectives and procedures are easily carried out. The volunteers get satisfaction from seeing a full unit of study carried to completion and they often receive a complete new vision of Early Childhood work. These people then become prime prospects for regular staff positions. There are also those who do have concern and ability but whose circumstances do not allow them to hold a permanent place on the teaching staff. Volunteering to work for a month in Church Time enables them to serve.

Having the same teachers together for the month benefits the children. They feel secure when familiar people are in charge of the program. This creates fewer discipline problems and more positive learning can take place. Replacing all but one teacher with volunteers for the church hour enables the Sunday School staff to attend church regularly.

Permanent Leader/Rotating Volunteers

The third plan combines several features of the first two. A permanent Church Time Leader serves with a different group of volunteer teachers each month. The Leader attends the Sunday School planning meeting to learn what will be happening the first hour, then briefs that month's volunteers on their assignments to insure a coordinated morning.

The success of this plan depends on the Sunday School staff's willingness to include the Church Time Leader as part of their team, and the Church Time Leader's willingness to follow the direction of the Sunday School Department Leader.

Both plans that use rotating volunteers depend heavily on parental cooperation. Usually, the first two volunteers recruited are parents of young children. By participating on this basis occasionally, parents can not only strengthen the church's program, they can also gain new ideas and skills by working with children other than their own alongside an experienced leader. Other groups to contact for volunteers include: high school and college groups, single adults and senior citizens.

CAUTION: A system of one-Sunday-a-month volunteers has not proven satisfactory in meeting children's educational and emotional needs. Also, asking teachers to permanently serve both hours may isolate some teachers from needed input, fellowship and learning at an adult level.

HOW LARGE A STAFF DO WE NEED?

Every department should always have a minimum of two adults in case of emergency. Departments with eight or less children need a leader and one teacher. Or, the two adults may choose to divide the Teacher and Leader tasks among them, sharing the necessary responsibilities for this size group. Departments with more than eight children need a leader and two or more teachers to maintain the proper teacher/pupil ratio. When a department has more than 15–18 children, a secretary is usually necessary. The age of the children involved determines both the teacher-child ratio and the maximum number of children in a department. Since five-year-olds don't need as much individual attention as babies, more five-year-olds can be in a room than infants.

SUGGESTED MAXIMUM SIZES
FOR EARLY CHILDHOOD DEPARTMENTS

0–1 year olds—12–15 children
2–3 year olds—16–20 children
4–5 year olds—20–24 children

Any departments that exceed these maximums should be divided to create two departments. When these suggested maximums are exceeded, teacher-child relationships suffer, behavior problems increase and learning efficiency decreases.

Because the relationships between teachers and children are the most important ingredients in a successful Early Childhood department, and because they provide the contact between the church and the home, a proper ratio of teachers to children must be maintained:

TEACHER-CHILD RATIOS

0–1 year olds—1 teacher per 4 children
2–3 year olds—1 teacher per 5 children
4–5 year olds—1 teacher per 6 children

A department with children whose age span covers more than two years should maintain the ratio suggested for the youngest children. The smaller ratio will allow more individual attention to meet the varied needs of each level of development.

HOW CAN WE GET ENOUGH TEACHERS

Once a church sees the need to maintain proper teacher-child ratios, the question of how to get enough teachers is invariably raised. Which is usually followed with the lament, "Nobody in our church wants to get involved!" When recruiting teachers seems to be a hopeless task, Ephesians 4:4-16 may be encouraging reading.

The apostle Paul lets us in on the magnificent truth that God has placed within the church all the resources needed to fulfill His mission in the world. Every group of believers in Christ, every congregation, possesses the gifts of ministry. No church needs to wait for someone to come from somewhere else to make the church effective. God has provided your church with the necessary people to get the job done. Your task is to discover and utilize those gifts.

Begin by meeting with the others in your church who share your concern for this ministry: your departmental staff, your division coordinator, the general superintendent and perhaps the pastor. Pray together that God will lead you to the right people, the people that He wants to use. Talk together about the positions needed to be filled and discuss people you know who are suited for the job. Then pray again.

When you have someone in mind, present their name to the responsible church board or officer for approval. Make an appointment to visit in the home of your prospect. Explain your purpose in calling. Clearly present the work of your department. Show curriculum materials to help the prospect understand the program. Tell him what would be expected in order to be effective and share why you feel he would be suited for this work. Ask the prospective teacher to observe next Sunday in the department. Then ask him to pray sincerely about it and make his decision on the basis of what he feels God would have him do.

Avoid making the job sound too easy. Teachers who are told there is not much to do usually end up not doing much! Close your visit with prayer. After observing, praying and thinking,

HERE IS ONE WAY TO RECRUIT TEACHERS...

RECRUITING TEACHERS A BETTER WAY

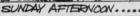

the prospect should have clearly in mind what lies ahead. The person who declines may still be a prospect for the future as the Lord continues to lead him. The person who accepts will be more likely to follow through on his commitment because he knows what to expect.

**GROUPING CHILDREN IN THE
EARLY CHILDHOOD DIVISION**

...when the attendance numbers less than:

5	30	50	80	110	220
You need 1 department of children...	You need 2 departments of children...	You need 3 departments of children...	You need 5 departments of children...	You need 6 departments of children...	You need 12 departments of children...
			Babies	Babies	Babies
	0–1 years	0–1 years	Toddlers	Toddlers	Toddlers
			2's	2's	2's 2's
0–5 years		2–3 years	3's	3's	3's 3's
	2–5 years		4's	4's	4's 4's
		4–5 years	4–5 years		
			5's	5's 5's
...with 1 department leader and 1 teacher	...with 2 department leaders, 2–5 teachers	...with 3 department leaders, 3–10 teachers	...with 5 department leaders, 5–16 teachers	...with 6 department leaders, 6–22 teachers	...with 12 department leaders, 12–44 teachers

HOW MANY DEPARTMENTS DO WE NEED?

Once a church knows how many teachers it needs for the number of children that attend—and what the maximum department sizes should be for each age level, it is time to decide how many departments are needed. The answer may get complicated by several factors. For instance, since young children need 25-35 square feet of space, many rooms may not be large enough to accommodate the maximum group sizes. Thus, a church with rooms smaller than 800 square feet would need more departments with fewer children each than a church with larger rooms.

Assuming that a church has 1) Adequate space to accommodate maximum group sizes; and 2) Approximately the same number of children in each age group, the following chart indicates the number of departments—and staff—needed as attendance grows.

STOP! Before continuing, do the following:

1. Determine the total number of children ages birth through five attending your Sunday School.

2. Determine the number of children of each age level in this total attendance.

The figures you now have will provide the basis for the number of departments that could best serve your Sunday School. Find where your Sunday School attendance fits in relation to the figures given in the following paragraphs. Then refer to the specific sections as directed.

If the total number of children attending is less than 30, read Section 1.

If the total number of children attending is between 30 and 49, read Section 2.

If the total number of children attending is between 50 and 79, read Section 3.

If the total number of children attending is 80 or over, read Section 4.

While we plan for the present, it also helps to look toward the future. If you anticipate an increased attendance because of outreach programs within the next few years, refer to the section

following the one recommended for your present attendance.
After you have read the section recommended for the attendance of your Early Childhood departments, proceed to the section entitled "How Should We Grade?"

Section 1:

Churches with less than 30 children in attendance between the ages of birth and five should plan two Early Childhood departments with the babies and toddlers grouped together in one department and the rest in another.

If there are five or less children, it may be temporarily necessary for these children to be in the same room as the infants and toddlers. Be sure babies and toddlers have a safe area of their own. One or two simple learning activities should be included for the older group during the morning.

A teacher should take the threes, fours and fives sometime during the morning to a quiet area of the room and present the Bible story. Include a few songs and finger fun. The two-year-olds and toddlers may gradually join the group, especially during the songs and finger fun.

Section 2:

Churches with 30 to 49 children need three Early Childhood departments. Once total attendance exceeds 30 and is distributed evenly between the age groups, a department for babies and toddlers, a department for twos and threes and a department for fours and fives will provide effectively for all children. One church with a large number of babies and toddlers found it helpful to have babies up to 18 months in one room, children up to three and a half years in the second and older threes in with the fours and fives.

Section 3:

Churches with a total attendance of 50 to 79 children between the ages of birth and five will need four or five Early Childhood departments. Again department divisions should be determined to provide balanced group sizes. The young child's need to be in a group where individual needs can be met should take precedence over adult desires to have uniform age division.

Section 4:

If your church has an attendance of 80 or more children between the ages of birth and five, you need a minimum of six Early Childhood departments.

HOW SHOULD WE GRADE?

The process by which a child is assigned to a particular department, and by which he moves on to the next department, is known as grading. Babies and toddlers should be promoted by developmental levels. A baby can be promoted from infants to creepers when he begins to crawl (around six months). Promotion to the toddler department coming when he can walk confidently without help (12-15 months). Toddlers can be moved in with two-year-olds at either two years, three months or two years, six months.

From this point, the most generally satisfactory method for grading in the Early Childhood department is by age, following the public schools plan to determine a child's eligibility for entrance into kindergarten or first grade. December 1 is the most common birthday used. For example, if a child reaches his fifth birthday on or before December 1, he may enter kindergarten the previous September.

A grading plan for the Early Childhood division usually requires that one department serves as a "holding department." A "holding department" receives new children throughout the year on their birthdays. Children remain in this department until the next regularly scheduled promotion day. Thus, the holding department will be small at the start of the year, and grow in size with each new arrival.

Teachers in the holding department should be aware of the wide range of abilities and needs of the children in the department. They should provide activities that will be of interest to the new children as well as challenging the older ones. It may be necessary to add an extra teacher to provide more personal attention. Twos and threes are the most common ages used in holding departments, allowing subsequent promotions to coincide with the rest of the Sunday School.

Learning to Organize and Use Materials

THE LEARNING ENVIRONMENT

Young children work, play and learn with their whole bodies. They require rooms equipped for action. Open space, child-sized equipment, and safe, interesting materials make a child feel his room at church is a good place to be. When the child feels this way, teachers can effectively accomplish their Bible teaching ministry.

Young children need to move, and movement requires space. Each child needs a minimum of 25 to 35 square feet (7.5 to 10.5 sq. m.) of space. Multiply the number of children in your room by 35 (or 10.5). Your answer represents the number of square feet (or meters) your room should contain. To determine how many children your present room can adequately handle, first measure the length and width of your room. Multiply these two measurements. Divide the answer by 35 (or 10.5). What is the child capacity of your room? How does this number compare with your attendance?

Rectangular-shaped rooms (about three-fourths as wide as they are long) provide more flexibility in room arrangements than a square or a long, narrow one.

When building or remodeling facilities for Early Childhood departments, it is strongly recommended that churches build all rooms with nine hundred to one thousand square feet per room.

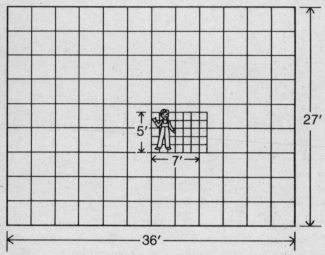

The idea of 25 to 35 square feet per person can be understood as an area 5x7 feet for each child. (Or 7.5 to 10.5 sq. m. per person is an area 1.5x2.1 m. for each child.)

This size room will accommodate the maximum attendance for five-year-old children, and will allow needed extra space per child should the rooms be used for younger groups.

The ideal *location* for all Early Childhood departments is at ground level, with quick and easy access to a safe outside area. Rooms on the first floor allow efficient safety precautions as well as convenience for parents. When teachers take children out of doors, they can do so with a minimum of confusion.

Select a *floor covering* that is durable and easy to clean. Vinyl tile in a subdued pattern is very satisfactory. Washable carpeting provides a quiet, relaxed atmosphere and is well worth considering. A rug on which children sit for group activities should be provided if a room has a hard, cold floor. The floor should be thoroughly cleaned after each session, especially in rooms for babies, toddlers and twos.

Ceilings covered with acoustical tile help deaden sounds;

walls also should be soundproof. *Windows* of clear glass, with the bottom sill two feet (60 cm) from the floor, provide children with a backdrop of God's Wonders. No window covering is usually necessary except to reduce glare and provide insulation.

Toilet facilities that immediately adjoin each room are desirable for children over two, and essential for babies and toddlers. A sink and a child-level drinking fountain in the department are also good investments. When a room has no sink, several plastic dishpans and pitchers should be available for use with activities requiring water.

Electrical outlets equipped with safety plugs and out of children's reach should be provided on each wall to avoid the hazards of extension cords.

Active young children need a *room temperature* between 68 and 70 degrees farenheit (or 21 degrees celsius). A thermometer hung about three feet (90 cm) from the floor can easily be checked. Radiators must be covered for safety. Adequate ventilation is also a must, for a room of active children can get stuffy very easily, thus making children restless and uncomfortable. Check for possible drafts from doors and windows.

Lighting should be even and without glare in all parts of the room. Soft pastel wall colors help to create a warm, cheery atmosphere—so vital to the welfare of young children. For rooms which are gloomy on darker days, use a soft yellow or pink wall color. To reduce glare in a sunny room, select a pale blue or green color. Bright colors can be added as highlights, but should not overpower bulletin board displays and other teaching tools.

Bulletin board space is desirable for visualizing the theme for a unit of lessons, and for displaying decorations children help prepare and arrange. One large bulletin board hung 18 inches from the floor should be placed as a backdrop in the area where children gather for Together Time. Other boards may be placed in activity areas to display related materials. Avoid cluttering the walls with unnecessary decorations. Only pictures related to the unit of study and children's current art work should be displayed. A "Parents' Board" should be mounted in the hallway and kept current with information related to the current unit.

To renew unsightly bulletin boards, cover entire surface with colorful burlap.

Ample *storage space* in each department is necessary. Much money is wasted when curriculum materials are not systematically stored, when scissors are lost and when paintbrushes are not put away. For teacher's materials, build cabinets mounted about 50 inches (125 cm) from the floor. This installation frees the floor space below the cabinets, making more room for children's learning activities.

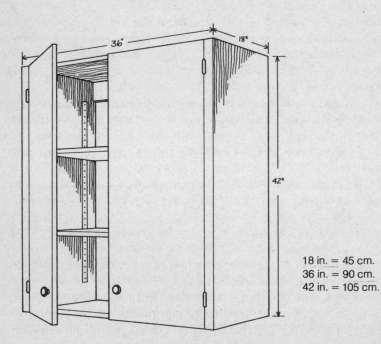

18 in. = 45 cm.
36 in. = 90 cm.
42 in. = 105 cm.

For displaying and storing children's materials and equipment, low, open shelves have proven most successful. Children can see what materials are available, can help themselves, then can return materials to shelves.

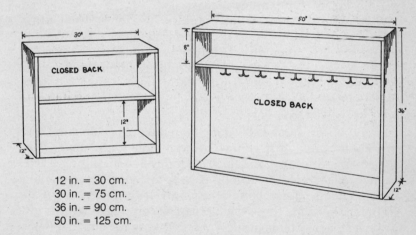

12 in. = 30 cm.
30 in. = 75 cm.
36 in. = 90 cm.
50 in. = 125 cm.

Avoid a bin to throw things in. A box or a bin with materials thrown in haphazardly is perhaps the poorest kind of storage unit. Children see chaos rather than an orderly display of materials; materials become lost, torn and soiled. Often children want to climb inside a box or bin, thus creating a safety hazard.

Coatracks for both children and adults are necessary pieces of equipment. The racks should include a place to store gloves, purses, Bibles, etc. When space is limited coat hooks and a shelf can be mounted on the wall, either in the room or in the hall outside your department door.

A *secretary's desk or counter* is helpful at the door. All department records and forms should be kept in neat order for efficiency in receiving children and securing needed information.

Your room does not need to be completely or perfectly furnished for effective learning to begin. Once you staff a room with several loving, concerned teachers and a few pieces of basic equipment for children's firsthand learning experiences, you're ready for action! Because limited budgets often force department leaders to acquire equipment one piece at a time, it is vital that a well-thought-out set of priorities be established so that the most necessary things are purchased first.

High on this list are the items children use for informal learning, such as a good set of unit building blocks. In selecting equipment, it is often wiser to buy fewer but better-made items than several stamped, metal ones. Order catalogs from several educational equipment supply firms for equipment ideas. Equipment of superior quality is well worth the investment in terms of years of hard wear.

Many times churches become the recipients of donated cast-offs. These materials may have been suitable for home play, but frequently are not appropriate in a Sunday School setting. Thank the donor, saying, "We'll look it over and pass it on to other children if it is not something the children are able to use in this setting." Then give these to an organization which repairs toys for reuse by charitable groups. When asking for donated items, be very specific in describing the materials needed.

Organize furnishings to form several centers or areas. Each area is furnished to facilitate the special learning that will take place there. This kind of arrangement is worth considering for several reasons:

First, children can use materials without interfering with those involved in other activities. Then a shy child, or one who is accustomed to working alone, can orient himself more quickly in a small area with a clearly defined focus and not have to relate to other children immediately upon entering the room.

Thirdly, the outgoing child who is easily overstimulated usually works more purposefully in a room arranged into centers. The arrangement of a room can invite pandemonium or it can suggest that it is a place where children are expected to be constructively occupied in learning.

Specific materials and equipment required for each area of the room are discussed in detail when each activity is described later in this chapter.

EQUIPMENT FOR BABIES AND TODDLERS

A room used for infants in cribs needs the following additional equipment: safe and sturdy, space-saving cribs, for each child (see sketch), one or two playpens of lightweight, easy-to-clean nylon, one or two adult rocking chairs, enamel carts or built-in changing tables, small refrigerator, electric bottle warmers and diaper bag storage, out of the child's reach.

Clean sheets for each crib each week are a must; also soft slippers for the teachers to wear in the room. (High heels are dangerous with creeping babies.) If teachers wear smocks, these

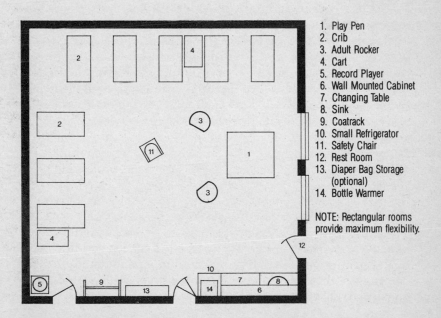

1. Play Pen
2. Crib
3. Adult Rocker
4. Cart
5. Record Player
6. Wall Mounted Cabinet
7. Changing Table
8. Sink
9. Coatrack
10. Small Refrigerator
11. Safety Chair
12. Rest Room
13. Diaper Bag Storage (optional)
14. Bottle Warmer

NOTE: Rectangular rooms provide maximum flexibility.

must be washed after each session. Warm crib covers, extra or disposable diapers and wastebaskets are also necessary.

Near the changing table or on shelves out of the child's reach keep washcloths or sponges, terry and paper towels, tissues, plastic bags and wax paper, cotton balls, baby oil and extra safety pins. Use plastic or paper containers rather than glass. Place the baby on a square of wax paper to change him, then wrap the soiled diaper in the wax paper or in a plastic bag. If there is a bowel movement, do not dispose of the stool but retain for the mother. Provide washable cuddle and squeeze toys, rattles, books and simple colorful pictures. Check all toys regularly to be sure they are in safe condition, with no parts that could be swallowed. Toys, bed rails and playpen rails need to be sterilized after each use. Check with your druggist about a safe, effective sterilizing solution.

A room for babies who are crawling does not require a crib for every child, since some will prefer to be in a playpen, on the floor or on a teacher's lap for much of the session. When a crib is used by more than one child during the morning, sheets must be changed and rails sterilized between uses. Other equipment includes: two playpens, several jumper chairs and low chairs with attached tables. Toys include those for younger babies, as well as lightweight pull and push toys, balls, simple containers which can be nested and filled.

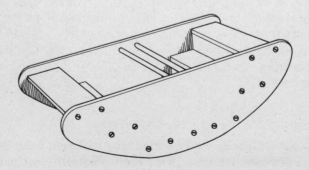

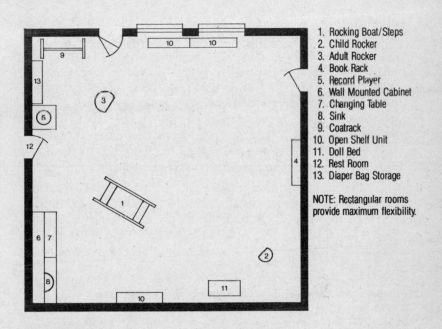

1. Rocking Boat/Steps
2. Child Rocker
3. Adult Rocker
4. Book Rack
5. Record Player
6. Wall Mounted Cabinet
7. Changing Table
8. Sink
9. Coatrack
10. Open Shelf Unit
11. Doll Bed
12. Rest Room
13. Diaper Bag Storage

NOTE: Rectangular rooms provide maximum flexibility.

In preparing a room for toddlers, separate them completely from the babies either by having separate rooms or substantial room dividers.

The room needs: a few cribs, a changing table, an adult rocking chair, one child-size table (chairs are optional), a doll bed (sturdy enough for children to climb into) and blankets, a rocking boat/climbing steps unit and cardboard or fabric blocks. Toys to add to the toddler room include several sturdy ride-on toys, stacking and nesting toys, and several dolls with molded plastic heads.

EQUIPMENT FOR TWOS THROUGH FIVES

Rooms for children over two look very different from those for babies and toddlers. Areas of the room are more clearly defined, specialized equipment and furniture have been introduced, and a wider variety of learning materials are available. However, the rooms still need to have considerable open space.

Chairs should be from 10-14 inches (25-35 cm) from the floor depending on the height of the children using them. Select chairs that are sturdy and not easily tipped over, but light enough for children to move. No adult-sized chairs are needed (except for secretary) since adults should work at the child's eye level. To avoid the confusion of moving chairs have children sit on rug for Together Time. The seating area on the floor can be defined with masking tape placed in a semicircle. "Sit on the line" is an easier instruction for children to follow than "make a circle." When space is limited, eliminate unnecessary chairs.

Tables should be 18-22 inches (45-55 cm) high, 10 inches (25 cm) higher than the chairs. The tabletop, durable and washable,

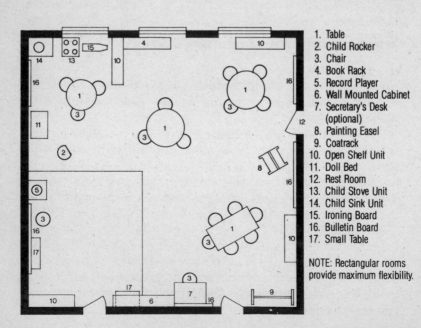

1. Table
2. Child Rocker
3. Chair
4. Book Rack
5. Record Player
6. Wall Mounted Cabinet
7. Secretary's Desk (optional)
8. Painting Easel
9. Coatrack
10. Open Shelf Unit
11. Doll Bed
12. Rest Room
13. Child Stove Unit
14. Child Sink Unit
15. Ironing Board
16. Bulletin Board
17. Small Table

NOTE: Rectangular rooms provide maximum flexibility.

should be approximately 30"x48" (75x120 cm). Avoid large tables that seat more than six. Select tables that allow the teacher to be within arm's reach of all children. Round tables have the advantages of being "friendly" and of having no corners. They are more expensive than rectangular tables which are more efficient work areas, especially for art projects.

ACTIVITIES FOR LEARNING

Having organized the room in a manner that is inviting to children and having provided materials appropriate to their age level for them to use, the teacher must become involved with the children as they explore and experiment. The child is ready to learn. Now is the time to put your curriculum to work. When the child arrives he chooses from the Bible Learning Activities offered. These experiences add "doing" to what a child is hearing and seeing throughout the morning. The activities involve the child in playing out familiar experiences of his home-centered world. Touching, smelling, tasting and experimenting at the God's Wonders table help the child experience interesting things God made. Becoming a member of the "family" at the Home Living area helps him practice ways of "obeying parents." Sharing materials during an art activity gives meaning to the verse "share with others" (1 Tim. 6:18, TLB).

Bible Learning Activities give the teacher assigned to each activity an opportunity to discover the child's level of understanding, what the child already knows about Bible truths and what misunderstandings he might have. This knowledge helps the teacher plan effectively to meet the needs of the individual child.

A young child learns through relationships. During Bible Learning Activities the teacher can work with the child on a one-to-one or one-to-two or three relationship. It is a time when the child gets to know the teacher and the teacher gets to know the child. Understanding comes through these shared experiences.

The following pages present a variety of Bible Learning Activities. The materials needed for each activity plus ways to accomplish specific Bible learning aims through these activities are included. Guidance is given about the age-level appropriateness of each activity.

Block Building

Provide opportunities for block building during Bible Learning Activities (Sunday School) and Choosing Time (Church Time).

Blocks are important learning tools for toddlers through fives, both boys and girls. Blocks help a child develop physically, mentally, socially and spiritually. Building with blocks allows him to work alone, parallel with another child or in cooperation with others in a small group. Lifting and carrying blocks helps satisfy his need for large muscle activity. Block building helps him to develop his own ideas and to make decisions. A child's imagination allows his blocks to become a car, a train, a house or a fire station. He also learns responsibility in caring for materials.

When the child works in small groups, block building provides him with opportunities for cooperation and sharing. He learns to respect the rights and ideas of others. He has opportunities for problem solving and decision making. Block building provides firsthand experiences in practicing Christian concepts, such as sharing, helping, taking turns and exercising self-control. Provide enough blocks so several children can enjoy block building at the same time.

Block building provides the teacher assigned to that area opportunities to relate the lesson's Bible teaching/learning aim to the child's interests and activities. At the block area she can occasionally initiate building projects to help children become familiar with Bible-time life. For instance, on a Sunday when a house will be mentioned in the Bible story, the teacher may show a picture of a Bible-time house, guide children in building one from blocks and pretending to "walk" people up to the roof. She familiarizes them with the idea of a flat-roofed house, so when they hear it mentioned in the story later in the morning, they can listen with understanding.

The child's use of blocks and other materials depends upon his maturity, his familiarity with the materials and his previous experiences. Expect a toddler or two-year-old to hold a block or carry one around with him. He may hold one in each hand and bang them together. He may pile one block on top of another and knock them down. A two-year-old may use blocks as steps or place them end to end so he can walk on them. He is learning how blocks feel and what he can do with them.

A three-year-old often uses several blocks at a time. He may stack them merely for the pleasure of stacking or he may attach a name to what he is building. The pile of blocks becomes whatever the child names it, changing its identity from moment to moment.

The four-year-old and five-year-old child is beginning to plan what he will build and how he will build it. He uses his imagination as he becomes involved in playing out an event with his construction. He enjoys using accessory toys such as boats and trucks in his block building. The five-year-old is beginning to put realism into his work. His work may take on the shape of a building with walls, doors, windows and a roof. He can be encouraged to build more realistically through suggestions, such as "What do you need in your building so the people can get inside?"

Materials ■ *Blocks:* Toddlers enjoy using large, soft fabric blocks. Both toddlers and twos work well with large, hollow cardboard blocks. Blocks for children under three should be lightweight and easy to manipulate. Suitable blocks can be made from empty milk cartons and cardboard boxes. These cartons and boxes may be stuffed tight with wadded newspapers, then covered with adhesive-backed paper. Threes are interested in building more complex projects; they need blocks of various shapes and sizes. A set of unit blocks, in which all block sizes are based on correlated measurements (two blocks of one size equal one block of the next size, etc. See sketch.) is a versatile learning tool that stimulates creative building. Since four- and five-year-old children build quite ambitious structures, they need a larger number and variety of blocks.

Wooden blocks are durable and may be purchased in sets or made from scrap lumber. Carefully sand and varnish each piece. When wooden blocks show signs of wear they can be sanded and refinished. They will last many years and are worth the investment.

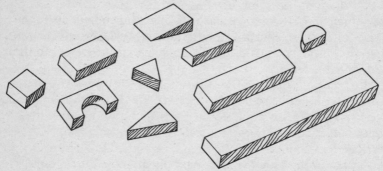

Standard size for the unit block is 2¾″ square, 1⅜″ thickness (6.9x3.45 cm).

Accessory toys: Toddlers and twos tend to use each toy—a block or a truck—independent of any other toys. However, these children will enjoy using accessory toys in the same area with the blocks. The value of block building is enhanced for the threes, fours and fives by a variety of accessory toys which encourage dramatic play.

Sturdy transportation toys should be a part of every block area. Wooden cars and trucks are preferable to most metal ones for safety and durability.

Other accessory toys include furniture and standup figures of people, animals and trees. These items can be purchased or made by gluing appropriate magazine pictures to pieces of wood or cardboard. Pieces of corrugated cardboard, 12″ x 12″ (30x30 cm), encourage the building of ramps, roofs, etc.

Fives and some fours enjoy using signs ("Airport," "Gas Station," "Church," etc.) in dramatic play. Signs should be printed in upper and lower case writing. Keep a felt pen and large index cards handy to make new signs.

Pictures: Occasionally, your Teacher's Manual will suggest the use of pictures to encourage children to build a specific object. Be alert for large, colorful pictures of boats, bridges, airplanes, etc., to add to your picture file.

Procedure ■ Blocks and accessory toys that are neatly arranged on low, open shelves invite the young child to build. Children can easily see what is available and can help themselves to the desired pieces. Establish the practice of stacking blocks by shape and size. Also, guide children to build several feet away from the block shelves so children may get to the blocks without knocking down someone else's construction. A strip of tape or a chalk line on the floor about two feet from the shelf serves as a silent reminder.

The floor in the block area should be carpeted with a smooth rug to provide a warm, level surface for building while at the same time reducing noise from falling blocks.

The child should be free to build what he wishes, setting the stage for relating his interest to the day's Bible learning aim. A teacher is nearby to offer guidance when needed.

Putting away blocks and accessory toys usually takes more time than other activities. Warn the children in advance that it's almost clean-up time. Guide children in stacking like-sized blocks together. Pieces of woodgrained adhesive-backed paper, cut the shape of the blocks and attached to shelves, will mark the place where each size block should be stored.

Bible Teaching/Learning Opportunities ■ How can the teacher use block building to relate the lesson aim and Bible Thoughts to a child's interest and experience? A teacher's conversation with young builders offers many opportunities to help children know and do what God's Word says.

Kindness/Sharing: As children work with blocks, identify specific acts of sharing and kindness. "Marie and Sharon. You girls are having such a good time playing together. You are sharing the blocks with each other. Our Bible says to share what you have with others." When introducing the Bible story later, remind children of specific acts you observed. "This morning I saw Jack do a kind thing for Ann. Jack moved over to give Ann room to build with blocks. I'm glad Jack was kind, and I'm glad I know a Bible story about a man who was kind."

Bible Thoughts for your conversation:
(Bible Thoughts indicating "See" with the reference have been edited for understanding by young children.)
"Share what you have with others." (See 1 Tim. 6:18.)
"Love one another." John 15:12
"Be kind to each other." Ephesians 4:32 *(TLB)*

Church: As several children worked with blocks, Mr. Cassidy began to sing, "Church Time, Church Time, Time to come to church." Becky looked up and smiled. "Becky, you look happy to be working and playing at church. Let's tell God we like to work at church." Becky and Mr. Cassidy bowed their heads. After they had both said, "Dear God, I like to work at church," Becky went happily back to her play.

Bible thoughts for your conversation:
Jesus said, "Come, learn of me." (See Matt. 11:28,29.)
"Come, let us worship the Lord." (See Ps. 95:6.)
"Be very glad." Matthew 5:12 (TLB)
"We love Jesus." (See 1 John 4:19.)

God's Wonders

Provide a God's Wonders display for Bible Learning Activities (Sunday School) and Choosing Time (Church Time).

Young children are bursting with curiosity! "Let me see!" (touch, taste, hear, smell) is their familiar plea. Discovery is an integral part of the young child's world. Exploring God's wonders helps a child begin to sense the extent of God's love, care and wisdom.

The wonder and excitement of nature presents a variety of opportunities to help the young child learn about God and himself. As he observes the wonder of seeds growing or a butterfly struggling out of its cocoon, simply say, "All things were made by God" (see John 1:3). When he sees the beauty in the design of a single snowflake, he can respond naturally by saying, "Thank you, God, for making snowflakes." Your conversations help the child learn to associate God with these experiences.

The presence of nature materials often seems to help an insecure child feel more comfortable in a new situation. If there is a live animal at the display, the child often focuses his interest on the animal and forgets himself. Babies enjoy looking at and touching a flower or a leaf. A goldfish's movements may fascinate a child. Introduce babies to living items one at a time— always kept in the teacher's hand.

The toddler or two-year-old will approach the God's Wonders display in a very simple way. At first he may pick up an object, look at it from all angles and maybe try to taste it. (Avoid pebbles, seeds and other things which may be small enough to swallow, and supervise carefully when plant leaves may be tasted!) Then he may put the object down and move on to another activity.

Expect him to return to the table several times during the morning and repeat the procedure.

The three-year-old continues to explore the wonders of God's world with increased interest. He is curious about living and growing things. He asks questions. He continues using his senses as a means of discovery.

Most fours and fives can participate in activities lasting for several weeks. These activities might include growing plants from seeds or watching a caterpillar change into a butterfly.

Materials and Procedures ■ Materials can be effectively displayed on a low shelf or table, near a window if possible. Growing plants or a simple aquarium are ever-changing sources of wonder. Living animals and birds, seasonal surprises such as autumn leaves and seeds, a pan of snow, icicles, shells, and flowers offer a child a firsthand experience in investigating God's wonders for himself. A good quality magnifying glass, a magnet and a Viewmaster of color slides of nature scenes are worthwhile additions to your God's Wonders display.

Have simple books about rocks, shells, animals, birds, reptiles, etc., clearly and accurately illustrated for a readily available source of information as you guide children in discovering God's Wonders.

Nature walks: Use a walking rope to keep children together. (A walking rope is a length of rope with knots tied 2 feet [60 cm] apart. The children hold onto it as they walk. Explain clearly and simply its purpose so children know what they are expected to do.) Bring containers for any specimen you find along the way. To make your walk a valuable learning experience, suggest something specific the children can look for. Remind children to choose things already on the ground—not leaves, flowers, and grasses that are still growing.

As you walk along, talk about the things you see. Avoid hurrying the children. Stop for a closer look at flowers, an insect or a rock. Relate what the children see to the orderliness of God's world, His care for the things He has made. "God planned for many trees to lose their leaves in the fall. In the spring the trees will grow new leaves."

Planting: Interesting indoor gardens can be grown from parts of fruit and vegetables. Save the top inch of carrots, beets, turnips or rutabagas. Stand the tops in a shallow dish of water. Use small pebbles to support the plant. Within a few days small white roots will appear and fern-like leaves will begin to grow. Seeds that will grow quickly are grass, lettuce, radish, lima bean, lentil, nasturtium, pumpkin, melon and marigolds.

Use unbreakable, wide bottom containers for planters. You will also need a supply of planter mix or soil and newspapers; watering cans. An important accessory in a planting experience is a magnifying glass.

Place a sweet potato, pointed end down, in a jar of water. Use a transparent plastic or glass container so roots will be visible. Leave about one-third of the potato above water. Insert several toothpicks if necessary to keep the potato from sinking. The potato will root and in about 10 days vines will begin to grow. Avocado seeds and onions can be planted in a similar way. Avocados may take up to 3 months to sprout—be patient! They grow into beautiful plants.

Some seeds can be planted so the children can see them germinate. Roll a piece of paper towel and put it inside a glass. The paper should touch the sides of the glass. Then fill the center of the glass with damp sand. Slip several lima beans between the paper and the glass (see sketch). Keep the sand moist. The children will have a clear view of the roots and root hairs.

For a hanging garden, cut an orange in half and scoop out the inside. Poke three holes near the rim with an ice pick to string yarn through for a hanger. Let the children spoon potting soil into the orange halves, then sprinkle grass seed on top or plant three sprouting lima beans. Beans may be "planted" first in egg cartons between pieces of soaking wet cotton. Allow a few days for them to sprout.

Magnets: Have a horseshoe magnet and two bar magnets available for four- and five-year-old children to use.

Provide a variety of objects, some of which will adhere to the magnet and some that will not. Also have two boxes, one marked yes and one marked no. Place a variety of objects in a shallow box or on the table. The child can experiment to see what the magnet will or will not attract. Objects the magnet attracts are placed in the box marked yes. "Did the magnet attract the paper clip? ...God planned for magnets to attract objects made of iron or steel."

For further experiments provide a piece of heavy paper, a glass or jar of water, a small pane of glass (bind the edges of the glass with masking tape to prevent cut fingers), a handkerchief, a dish of sand or dirt and paper clips. Ask, "Will the magnet attract through a piece of paper? ...Let's find out." Lay a piece of paper over a paper clip. Use the magnet to lift the paper clip and paper. Repeat the experiment using the pane of glass. Lay the paper clip on top of the paper or pane of glass. Let a child hold the magnet underneath. As the child moves the magnet the paper clip will move. Let a child pick up a paper clip or other iron object with a magnet wrapped in a handkerchief or use a magnet to retrieve a paper clip from a glass of water.

Children enjoy playing games involving magnets. For "Find the Nail" provide drinking straws, three or four large finishing nails and toothpicks.

Place a nail in each of three or four straws. Place toothpicks in the remaining straws. Bend the ends of the straws to keep the nails and toothpicks from falling out. Place the straws in a box.

The children take turns using the magnet to find the straws containing nails.

Water: Water play is an ideal outdoor activity. However, with proper protection of the floor and tabletops, water play can be a successful indoor activity as well. A large sheet of plastic will protect floors and carpets; newspapers will protect tabletops.

An apron, a small container such as a sandpail of water and a wide brush are all the equipment needed for the young child to experiment with water painting. He can paint outside walls, sidewalks, outdoor equipment or large sheets of masonite.

Most children three and up enjoy blowing bubbles; it requires the simplest of equipment. Mix water with soap chips in paper cups. Give each child a cup of soapy water and a drinking straw. Demonstrate blowing air into the straw. Keep a sponge handy to wipe up spills. The children will also enjoy mixing the soapy water with a rotary beater. A few drops of food coloring will make colorful bubbles.

Moving their hands through water and slowly pouring water from one container to another seems to have a calming effect on most young children. They enjoy the feel and the fun of water. Provide a large plastic tub or basin of water and plastic eyedroppers, funnels, unbreakable measuring cups, squeeze bottles, and soup ladles. The children will experiment with pouring, measuring, squirting and washing. Some will be content to just wiggle their fingers in the cool water. (Bathing dolls, washing dishes and scrubbing tabletops is an excellent enrichment activity for the Home Living center.) "How does the water feel, Jan? I'm glad God made the cool water....Does this cup hold as much water as that cup, Eric? Which cup holds the most water? You're using the eyes God gave you to see how much water is in each cup."

For an experiment involving frozen water, give each child a paper cup containing one or two ice cubes. Talk about how the ice feels (cold, hard, wet, slippery) and of what the ice is made. "Who made the water?...All things were made by God!...What is ice? Ice is water that has been frozen solid. Why do we need ice?... What happens when ice is not in a refrigerator?'' Place the cups outside in the sunshine. At the end of the hour check to see what has happened to the ice.

Children enjoy experimenting with all kinds of objects to determine which objects float and which ones sink. Let the children take turns placing objects (some that float, some that sink—rock, cork, marble, sponge, twig, spoon, etc.) in a large container of water such as an aquarium. As each child puts his object in the water, ask, ''Will the (feather) sink or float?'' Objects sink when they are heavy enough to push aside the water in which they are placed. It is sufficient at this time to simply state, ''God made some objects to float and some to sink.'' Give brief, meaningful facts rather than a long, dull explanation.

Senses: For activities involving the sense of touch, provide babies and toddlers with blocks, balls or pillows covered with a variety of fabrics: satin, terry cloth, wool, fur, etc. Older children enjoy a ''feel walk,'' in which they take off their shoes and walk over a variety of textured materials and describe how each feels. Fours and fives may do the walk blindfolded.

Threes through fives enjoy reaching into a bag or box and identifying familiar objects only by feel. Twos and younger threes can do this if they see the objects before they are put in the bag. ''You guessed what that was just by using your fingers. I'm glad God made our fingers so we can feel with them.''

For activities involving sight, provide baby food jars half full of water. Guide the children in adding food coloring with water droppers make the color desired. It usually takes three drops for dark colors and more for yellow. Next try mixing colors. "Watch what happens when you squeeze a little blue into the yellow....What color is it now?...God made our eyes to see beautiful colors."

Play a color guessing game. Teacher sings (to the tune of "Here We Go Round the Mulberry Bush")

"Look around the room with me
The room with me, the room with me.
Look around the room with me.
I see something (red)."

The children take turns guessing various objects. The one who guesses correctly picks an object and whispers it in the teacher's ear. She sings the song, putting in the child's name: "Look around the room with (Sue), she sees something (blue)."

For activities involving hearing, use a cassette recorder to tape common household sounds: doorbell, phone, vacuum cleaner, pots and pans, etc. Play a sound for the children to identify. Give clues and replay sounds when necessary. Bring a tape recorder and tape the children singing or individuals talking; then play it back for them to hear. "Judy, I can hear your voice singing on the tape recorder. God gave us ears to hear."

Talk about various things children use their ears for at home, at church. "I like to listen to singing at church. It makes me happy to hear glad songs about Jesus."

Play a listening game for threes. Give one simple direction at a time: stand on one leg, put your hand on your head, touch your nose. Commend children for listening and following instructions.

For activities involving the sense of smell, make "I Can Smell" booklets. Saturate pieces of felt with aromas, such as peppermint, clove, lemon, perfume, etc. The child glues the felt inside a folded sheet of paper to make a booklet. Children smell each other's booklets to identify odors.

For activities involving taste provide bit-sized pieces of fruit and vegetables. With fours and fives, blindfold one child at a time, giving him one thing to taste and identify. Ask children, "Is it sweet or sour? Is it warm or cold?"

Animal Life: There is a wide variety of animal life that can be brought into the classroom. Animal friends can range from insects and tadpoles to a child's pet. In the summer you can make an earthworm farm. Put a quart jar inside a gallon jar. Fill the smaller jar with sand to weight it down. Fill the space between both jars with loose, damp soil and five or six large worms. Put black paper around the outside of the larger jar for a week. In the darkness the worms behave as if they are underground. When you take the paper off the next Sunday, you will be able to observe tunnels the worms have made. Keep the dirt moist by adding a little water each week.

Insects, such as caterpillars, can be kept in large jars with air holes in the lid. Leaves from the tree on which they were found should be included. Food needs vary. Ladybugs eat aphids. Crickets eat bread crumbs, raisins and lettuce. Grasshoppers thrive on leaves, bread crumbs and even orange peels. All insects need water.

Fish are easy to care for in a bowl or aquarium. Provide commercially packaged fish food. Birds such as parakeets or canaries are also excellent visitors to Sunday School departments.

Place the insect, animal or bird in an area where the children can view it easily. As the children watch, call their attention to specific things about the insect or animal. "See how the toad flicks out his tongue to catch his food. God made the toad's tongue in a very special way.... The caterpillar is beginning to spin his cocoon. He is spinning the thread round and round his body just as God planned." Children can share in the care of animal life by helping clean cages, bringing food and feeding the animal with the teacher's guidance. After a few Sundays of observance, the insects and animals should be returned to their natural habitats.

Bible Teaching/Learning Opportunities ■ The child's natural interest and curiosity in God's Wonders provides endless opportunities for the teacher to help him know what God's Word says and how it relates to his life.

Creation: Plants, elements or weather, and animals are quite easily related to lessons on creation. Other activities at the God's Wonders table can be related to creation also. It is God who made the hands to feel, the ears to hear, etc. Magnetism, and refraction of light in a prism and the ability of water to support weight are all part of God's creation.

"What are you using to smell the lemon, Jack? God made our noses so we can smell lemons and flowers and all kinds of things. All things were made by God.... What do the plants need to grow? God made the sun and rain to help the plants grow."

Bible Thoughts for your conversation:
"God made everything beautiful." (See Eccles. 3:11.)
"The Lord has done great things for us." Psalm 126:3
"God gives rain on the earth." (See Job 5:10.)

Thankfulness: Young children respond naturally to the wonder and awe of God's creation. This response of mind and heart easily becomes one of thankfulness. "How does the rain help us? God gives rain on the earth. We can tell God thank you for the rain....I thank God for our eyes. Tell us one thing you can see with the eyes God gave you....This cool water feels good on a hot day like today. We can tell God thank you for the water. Our Bible tells us it is good to give thanks to the Lord."

Bible Thoughts for your conversation:
"I thank God." 2 Timothy 1:3 *(TLB)*
"Give thanks to the Lord, for He is good." Psalm 136:1
"It is good to sing praises to our God." Psalm 147:1

Books

Provide a quiet area where children can look at books during Bible Learning Activities (Sunday School) and Choosing Time (Church Time). Books may also be used occasionally to supplement other activities and during Together Time.

Books are important learning tools for all children. They bring pleasure, create ideas, stimulate curiosity and help children solve problems. Books help the young child develop an awareness of words. They provide opportunities for close physical contact between a teacher and child. Happy experiences with colorful, interesting books help create a desire to read.

Children enjoy looking at books alone or hearing the book read by the teacher. Books for young children are most effective when they reinforce firsthand learning experiences. Books about familiar objects and events are best.

Babies and toddlers need books with simple, colorful and realistic pictures. The teacher of babies should make very simple comments about the pictures. With toddlers, ask the child to point to items as you name them.

Twos and threes are still primarily interested in the pictures. The child will often point to one object in a picture and name it. Although younger children are usually anxious to go on to the next page, they enjoy responding to simple questions about the picture. Teachers can help build vocabulary by repeating the child's reply in a complete sentence and sometimes adding a descriptive word. "What is this, Karen?...That's right. It's a cat. It's a yellow cat. God made the yellow cat."

Fours and fives look primarily at the pictures in a book, but also enjoy hearing a brief story. Select storybooks with no more than a few sentences per page. Many children are aware of the words on the page. A child may ask, "What does this word say?" Five-year-olds are learning to recognize some words and may happily announce, "I know that word! That word is 'stop.'"

Encourage fours and fives to use books for research. "There is a book about insects on our bookshelf. Let's see if it tells about this ladybug."

Materials ■ A good selection of books provides opportunities to widen a child's horizons to relate Scripture truth to his interest and experience. The books listed in your curriculum materials relate specifically to the Unit teaching/learning aim. Use these lists as your guide when you purchase books for your department. Select picture books with large, clear, colorful pictures and a minimum of detail.

Children enjoy making their own books, using magazine pictures or their own art. They will often return many times to look at books they helped put together. Books for babies and toddlers should be of cloth or vinyl to survive being chewed and pulled, and should be wiped or washed after use each week.

Books for twos and threes should have a few words on each page. Stories should be about familiar subjects, such as animals, babies and families; and about familiar activities, such as playing, helping, eating and sleeping. Books for fours and fives may also include pictures and stories about nature, machines and children from other lands. Simple stories about Jesus can be included for all ages.

A Bible is the most important book in the room. Provide a large Bible in which you have taped the pictures from the child's curriculum materials. Insert these pictures next to the appropriate Scripture passage. Use a red pen to lightly shade the story. Also mark verses used in conversation.

Procedure ▪ With babies, take a book to the crib or playpen to show the child. With toddlers and older children, display books where children can see and reach them. Limit the number of books you display; too many simply confuse a child. Three to five is a good number for toddlers and twos. Older children may use up to seven or eight. All books used should relate to the current unit of lessons.

Books should be attractively arranged in a quiet area of the room, where a child can browse through a book alone or join two or three others to listen to a story. Unless a teacher is nearby to read the text or talk about the picture, a child has "seen" a book in a few seconds.

As you look at a picture book with a child, ask questions that will stimulate observation and thought. "What sound does a dog make?... What is the kitten wearing around its neck?... Why do you think the girl looks sad?"

A book rack with slanting shelves is ideal for displaying a few books. It also provides space in the back for storing books not in use.

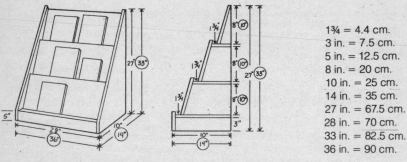

1¾ = 4.4 cm.
3 in. = 7.5 cm.
5 in. = 12.5 cm.
8 in. = 20 cm.
10 in. = 25 cm.
14 in. = 35 cm.
27 in. = 67.5 cm.
28 in. = 70 cm.
33 in. = 82.5 cm.
36 in. = 90 cm.

Circled figures are for 3s through 5s; others for toddlers and 2s.

Place an appropriate book at an interest center and encourage the children to use it for reference. "This book is about many different kinds of rocks. Maybe we can find a picture of our rocks in the book."

Use the picture Bible in the book area. Young children can know that the Bible is a special book that tells us about God and the Lord Jesus. They will enjoy looking through the Bible and recognizing pictures that illustrate a favorite story. Bible storybooks with clear, accurate pictures help children know of Bible-time customs, clothing, homes, etc.

Bible Teaching/Learning Opportunities ■ Sharing/Helping: When your lesson's Bible teaching/learning aim involves sharing, kindness or helping, select books with stories about children who demonstrate these kinds of behavior. In your conversation encourage the child to talk about what is happening in the story or pictures and relate the happenings to Scripture truth. "What is the boy doing?...When we rake the leaves we are helping. Our Bible tells us to help each other."

The use of books provides opportunities for children to share, to help and to be kind. "Mary, you are kind to move over so Kenny can see the book, too....Lisa, thank you for choosing this book. We will enjoy looking at it with you."

Bible Thoughts for your conversation:
"Children, obey your parents." Ephesians 6:1
"Always be kind to everyone." Galatians 6:10 (TLB)

Creation: When you use picture books about animals and nature for twos and threes, ask, "What do you see in this picture? Who made the puppy?... What is growing on the tree? (To give young children a clue, point to the object in the picture as you mention it.) God planned for apples to grow on trees."

As fours and fives use books to learn more about objects on the God's Wonders table, relate God to the illustrations in the book. "Bees carry pollen from flower to flower. God planned for bees to help new plants to grow.... The tiny sea animal that lived in this shell built his shell larger and larger as he grew. God planned it that way."

In the picture Bible point out Bible words that relate to creation. "This is the part of the Bible that tells us that God made our beautiful world. Right here it says 'God made the sky!...' See the words marked with red? They tell us that all things were made by God."

Bible Thoughts for your conversation:
"God made the world and everything in it." (See Acts 17:24.)
"God gives us all things to enjoy." (See 1 Tim. 6:17.)
"All things were made by God." (See John 1:3.)

Puzzles

"Look! I did it!" Scott shouts as he completes a puzzle. Puzzles help satisfy a child's desire to achieve. They provide an opportunity for the child to work alone or with one or two friends.

When a child uses puzzles he learns to think, to reason and to solve problems. He learns to work independently. Working puzzles helps develop eye-hand coordination. Through using puzzles a child can enjoy a sense of achievement. He learns to share and take turns. Puzzles also prepare them for learning to read. Help the children lay out the pieces on the left side of the puzzle to encourage using left-to-right eye coordination.

Materials ▪ Toddlers enjoy puzzles such as stacking rings and nesting boxes. Older toddlers and twos can succeed with flat puzzles with three or four pieces. Each puzzle piece is a picture of a whole object (a bunny, a ball, etc.). He will press the piece against the puzzle frame, maneuvering it until it falls into place. Threes, fours and fives can work puzzles with pieces that are parts of a whole object. The complexity of the puzzle used depends upon the child's coordination and dexterity, not necessarily his age. Wooden inlay puzzles are best for jigsaw because of their durability and ease of use. Puzzles for two-year-old children should have a maximum of 4-6 pieces; threes, 6-12 pieces; fours, 10-15 pieces; fives, 10-plus pieces. Each department should offer puzzles of varying degrees of difficulty to allow for the varying abilities of the children.

Puzzles should be colorful with simple, realistic pictures. Select puzzles that depict places and things familiar to children. A puzzle rack is a worthwhile investment. It helps keep puzzle pieces from becoming lost; children learn quickly to take only one puzzle from the rack at a time, and to put it back when they have finished.

If a piece is lost, make a replacement from plastic wood. Press aluminum foil into the place where the piece fits. Fill the foil with the plastic wood. When it dries, sand off any rough edges, then paint the piece.

Until you are able to purchase wooden puzzles, you can improvise by making puzzles yourself. Glue appropriate picture to a 12"x18" (30x45 cm) piece of Masonite. Apply weight while

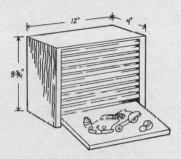

4 in. = 10 cm.
8¾ in. = 22.1 cm.
12 in. = 30 cm.

drying. Spray picture with clear plastic and let dry. Draw cutting lines on picture. Avoid cutting across faces. Divide into six or eight large pieces. Cut picture with coping saw. Sand all edges. Use a shallow 12″x18″ (30x45 cm) box, with lid, for storage and as frame in which child assembles puzzle.

Felt boards are an interesting puzzle variation. Cover a 10″x12″ (25x30 cm) piece of plywood with solid-colored felt. Cut objects such as geometric shapes, houses, churches, trains, trees, flowers, birds, butterflies, cats, dogs, boys, girls, etc., out of different types of material. (Wallpaper samples, satin, leather, sandpaper, velvet, fur.) Back them with felt. Children may make their own pictures with the figures. Encourage them to tell stories about their creations. Or you may play a matching game. The teacher or a child chooses a figure and places it on his board. The others find one with the same texture or color and put it in the same place on their board.

A unique kind of puzzle that captures the interest of young children is a gadget board. To make a gadget board, sand and shellac a 12″x48″x1″(30x120x2.5 cm) board. Along outer edges attach (with screws) hardware items commonly used about the house, such as door hook, slide lock, light switch, etc. Place gadget board on low table so several children at a time can use it.

Also include construction toys, peg boards and large beads for stringing.

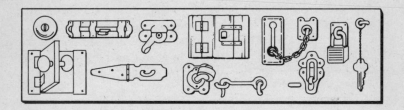

Procedure ■ As a child works puzzles over and over again he will gain confidence and be able to proceed to more complicated ones. Have a more difficult puzzle ready and waiting for that moment. "Allen, you completed that puzzle so quickly and so easily! I have a new puzzle for you. It's a little bit harder, but I know you can do it." Remain nearby to give encouragement. Praise the child's accomplishments.

If a child is becoming frustrated in his attempts to complete a puzzle, step in with suggestions that will allow him the satisfaction of completing the puzzle on his own. "I wonder if the piece will fit if you turn it around? ... This part of the puzzle is red. Can you find a red piece that will fit right here?"

Give the child the responsibility of returning the puzzle to its proper place when he is finished.

Bible Teaching/Learning Opportunities ■ Sharing/Helping: When your lesson's Bible teaching/learning aim involves "Sharing" "Kindness" or "Helping," select puzzles with pictures of children demonstrating these kinds of behavior. In your conversation encourage the child to talk about what is happening in the picture and relate the action to Scripture truth. "The girl in your puzzle is using her hands to help. What is she doing? God made our hands to help."

Working with puzzles gives children opportunities to share, to help and to be kind.

"Marilyn, thank you for sharing your puzzle with Paula. Our Bible tells us to share what you have with others...."

Bible thoughts for your conversation:

"Treat everyone with kindness." (See Gal. 6:10.)
"Serve the Lord with gladness." Psalm 100:2
"Do good things." (See Isa. 1:17.)
"Hear the Word of God and obey it." (See Luke 11:28.)

Church: During a unit of lessons that focuses on the church, provide several puzzles showing familiar church experiences. Talk about the scenes as well as other experiences children enjoy at church. If it is necessary to use some puzzles with other scenes, compare them with what is happening at church. "Eric, why does the boy in your puzzle look happy?...What are some things at our church that make you happy?"

Bible thoughts for your conversation:

"Come together in the church." (See 1 Cor. 11:18.)
"Bring a love gift." (See 1 Chron. 16:29.)
"We will gladly give." (See Judg. 8:25.)
"I am glad." John 11:15

Home Living

Provide Home Living activities for Bible Learning Activities (Sunday School) and Choosing Time (Church Time).

The Home Living area offers an environment in which young children can relive home experiences. These activities provide a natural setting where a teacher can relate Scripture truth to the children's interest and experience.

The Home Living area allows the young child to practice

Christian concepts, such as sharing, helping, taking turns and being kind. He can express thankfulness to God as he prays before eating his "pretend" meal or putting the baby to bed.

By listening and observing at the Home Living area, the alert teacher can gain new insight into what a child is feeling. The child's actions reveal clues to his interests, his abilities, how he sees himself, what things are bothering him and his understanding of concepts being taught.

The toddler and two-year-old may be content to simply rock the baby, feed the baby or put the baby to bed. They may want to be the baby, sitting in the toy high chair or lying in the doll bed. They play alone, each one involving no one else in his activity. Since their command of words is limited, they often use play as a means of expressing ideas.

During the years three, four and five, the child becomes more verbal and his play becomes more complex. He spends additional time at his play and needs extra "props" such as dress-up clothes and accessories. As he learns to interact with other children, those in the Home Living area adopt roles to become a "family." Familiar experiences are relived again and again.

Materials ■ Equipment for the Home Living area should be child-size rather than doll-size. A must for every Home Living area including toddlers is a doll bed, sturdy and large enough for a child to lay in, several blankets, and an assortment of dolls (include representatives of more than one race). Avoid dolls with hair (they usually become beauty parlor rejects within a short time) and dolls with mechanical features such as eye-blinking, wetting, walking, talking, etc. Add a wooden stove, and sink unit for twos through fives. Home corner furniture can be purchased from educational equipment firms or made from crates and boxes. Furnishings should include unbreakable dishes, empty food containers, pots and pans, a child-size broom and a telephone. Omit silverware or anything which suggests being put into small mouths.

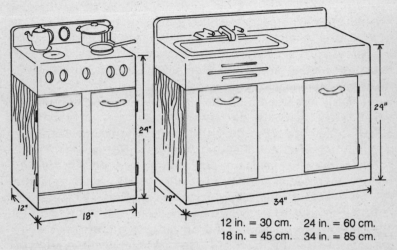

12 in. = 30 cm.   24 in. = 60 cm.
18 in. = 45 cm.   34 in. = 85 cm.

Dress-up clothes are an important part of Home Living play. Include dresses, men's and women's hats, scarves, jewelry, shoes and purses. Also men's jackets, hats, neckties, a briefcase, discarded camera, binoculars, toolboxes, lunch boxes, billfolds and keys.

Dressing up will be easier if clothing is about a fifty-grade child's size rather than adult, although shoes should be large enough to go over the child's shoes. Other equipment that may be provided includes doctor and nurse kits for playing hospital, as well as toy cash registers and play money for playing store.

Procedure ■ The teacher arranges the materials in the Home Living area before the children arrive. He then becomes an interested observer, moving into the activity to:

■ Suggest play ideas that provide natural connections to the lesson's Bible teaching/learning aim.
■ Relate the lesson's aim to the child's interest and activity.
■ Help a shy child enter the activity.
■ Settle a dispute or aid the children in solving a problem.
■ Insure the safety and well-being of the children.

Since dramatic play is free and spontaneous, the children will become involved as their needs and interests dictate. A special accessory and a suggestion from the teacher can guide the child's play toward a specific aim without interfering with the spontaneous dramatic play. For instance, a picture book might become the stimulus to "read" to the babies at bedtime, allowing conversation about the unit's Bible stories. A small overnight bag and a suggestion about taking a trip can initiate extended play and opportunities to talk about God's care wherever we go.

As you plan for Home Living activities, ask yourself, "How will this activity help accomplish the lesson's Bible teaching/planning aims?"

In addition to dramatic play, the Home Living area is often the scene of simple food preparation activities. Banana pudding, no-bake cookies, lemonade or cheese slices are easy and popular. Many cooking experiences can be provided using electric fry pans. As children work with a teacher, many opportunities are creative, for emphasizing helping and sharing or God's care and provision for us.

Bible Teaching/Learning Opportunities ■ A teacher can use the young child's natural interest in Home Living activities to build many Christian concepts.

Helping: The Home Living area provides many opportunities for helping. The "children" help "Mother" set the table. "Daddy" helps iron clothes. "Everyone is helping in our home today. We have happy homes when everyone helps. Our Bible reminds us that we...are helpers." Children who work at the Home Living area are responsible to help put away equipment. "Marcia knows just where to put the dishes...Cindy is helping to pick up the dolls...What hard work she is doing! I am helping tuck the dolls in bed. Our Bible says 'I will help.' "

Bible Thoughts for your conversation:

"I will help." (See 2 Sam. 10:11.)

"With love, help one another." (See Gal. 5:13.)

"Learn to help." Titus 3:14 *(TLB)*

Thankfulness: As children play out familiar activities they can be guided to respond quite naturally in thanks to God for food, family, home, church, friends, etc. "What do we do before we eat our dinner? Steve, you may tell God thank you for the good food....I saw a happy family in our 'home' today. God planned for us to have happy times with our families. We can tell God thank you for our families. Our bible tells us to be thankful to God."

Bible Thoughts for your conversation:

"I thank God." 2 Timothy 1:3

"Be thankful to God." (See Ps. 100:4.)

"It is good to give thanks to the Lord." Psalm 92:1

Art Activities

"What did you learn today in Sunday School?" Denise's mother asked. Soundlessly, Denise thrust a rumpled piece of paper at her mother. Denise hoped her art work could speak for her.

Art experiences are among the most familiar—and most misunderstood—in an Early Childhood department. Most young children are introduced to crayons very young, but few adults take the time to observe the child at work, to see the real values of what is being done. The key word in a young child's art experience is *process*—not *product*. The work the child puts into the experience is of more value than the finished product. The skills and attitudes and understandings a child gains far overshadow the price of paper that adults often make the object of much attention. The emphasis in this section is on providing enjoyable and meaningful art experiences for children to do, rather than on clever or beautiful art objects for them to make.

Art activities offer the young child an opportunity to give expression to what he thinks and feels. A happy, secure child may express his happiness through the bright colors he uses in his easel painting. A shy or inhibited child may express his feelings by making just a few timid strokes with one finger on his finger painting. An angry child may release his emotions by pounding, squeezing or twisting clay.

To help a child become more self-confident and sure of his worth as an individual, he needs a teacher who is friendly and understanding about his art work. As he works at art activities the child can learn basic Christian concepts of sharing, taking turns, being kind and helping others. He has opportunities to learn respect for the ideas and work of those about him.

As a child and teacher use art materials together in a relaxed, creative way, opportunities for natural conversation with the child are likely to come. These "teachable moments" often are the best opportunities to help a child learn basic and vital scriptural truths.

As in other areas of growth, the child progresses through a certain pattern of development in artistic expression. And, as in other areas of growth, he passes through these stages at his own speed.

The first stage in artistic development is called the manipulative stage. This stage begins when the child first begins to use crayons, paint or clay. It is a time of exploration; a time of manipulating materials. He discovers what happens when he moves a crayon across a piece of paper or squeezes a piece of clay. He discovers how the materials look, smell, feel and taste.

Toddlers through threes are usually in this manipulative stage of development. Most young children will return to this stage when introduced to new materials for the first time. A child's work should not be considered "babyish" nor should he ever be told to "Draw something nice. Don't just scribble!"

From the manipulative stage the child progresses to the controlled stage. He begins to realize that he has some ability to regulate his materials. He learns that he can use glue to make materials stick together; that clay can be patted into shapes or pinched into pieces. He learns that he can make a line go a certain direction by moving his crayon a certain way.

Next the child enters the naming stage. He completes a piece of work and announces, "See my doggy." At first, the adult may be able to see no resemblance between the object pictured and what the child says it represents. However, his skills are rapidly developing and eventually the resemblance will become apparent. Early in this stage the child begins to name his work *before* he does it. This intent to make a man, a flower, a house is a powerful impetus to his maturing skills.

The teacher's role is to encourage the child and help him feel pride in his creation at whatever stage he may be. Comments such as, "I like the bright colors in your picture, Greg," or "You certainly worked hard on your painting. You know about painting!" show your acceptance of a child's work.

Materials and Procedure ▪ When you introduce a new art activity, demonstrate the use of materials. Then remove your work. Some children might tend to copy your efforts and thus miss out on using their own creativity.

Painting: An apron or a smock is a must for all painting activities. An apron can be made from shower curtain materials. A smock can be made easily from a man's shirt. Cut off the sleeves to make them the right length for a child. The child wears the shirt backwards so it buttons in the back. Fix one large button and buttonhole so children can help each other. Since only a few children at a time will be painting, only several aprons or smocks are needed. Sponges and soapy water for cleanup are also necessary for all painting activities.

Be sure floor surface is washable. If it is carpeted, place a large plastic dropcloth or several thicknesses of newspaper on the floor in the painting area.

Materials for *finger painting* include finger paint and a smooth surface on which to paint. Finger paint may be purchased, but can also be made easily and inexpensively by mixing equal parts of liquid starch and soap flakes; add a few drops of detergent. Beat together till smooth. Then add tempera paint for color. Shaving cream and whipped soap flakes can also be used for finger painting. The surface on which to paint can be finger-paint paper, slick butcher or shelf paper, a formica or enamel tabletop, a large tray or a piece of oil cloth. One attractive feature of finger painting is that the entire creation can be wiped out in a moment if the child desires. Most children enjoy simply moving the paint around on a smooth surface and do not feel the need to make a picture.

If a child wants a picture to take home, lay a clean piece of paper over the finger painting, rub the paper lightly and pull it off.

Toddlers and twos can be introduced to finger painting. Work with one or two children at a time to avoid messes. Expect some children to be reluctant to try until they have watched others for a while.

Provide pans of warm, soapy water for cleanup. Let the child soak his hands in the water for a few minutes when his work is finished. His hands will come clean with very little scrubbing and he will enjoy the feel of the warm water.

For *easel painting*, provide paper, large brushes, liquid tempera, paint containers and easels. Paper should be 18"x24" (45x60 cm). Newsprint, manila, butcher paper and the want-ad section from the newspapers can all be used. Brushes should have long handles—about 10 to 12 inches (25 to 30 cm)—and wide, soft bristles. Liquid tempera paint, available from art supply stores or educational material firms, is convenient and easy to use. It can be thinned with water, liquid starch or liquid soap, if necessary.

Powdered tempera is less expensive to buy, but it is also less convenient, since it has to be mixed into a liquid. Powdered tempera can be mixed with water or liquid starch or a combination of both. The prepared mixture should be the consistency of heavy cream. A few drops of liquid soap added to the paint makes cleanup easier. Paint containers can include empty frozen juice or soup cans, baby food jars with screw tops or ½ pint milk cartons with the tops removed. The lids on baby food jars keep the paint from drying out overnight. Easels can be purchased in either wood or aluminum but substitutes can be made from cardboard, pegboard or Masonite. If necessary, the children can paint on tables or on walls protected against drips.

Twos should begin with only one color. As their experience with easel painting increases, the number of paints they use may increase. Fours and fives may use from six to eight colors, with a brush for each color. The child needs instruction on how to drag his brush along the edge of the container to prevent dripping, and to return the brush to the same color when he is through. The teacher may have to help the child understand that he paints on his paper, not on his hands, his neighbor, the walls, etc. Except for these instructions, the child should be allowed to paint what he wishes without interference.

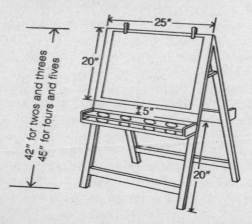

5 in. = 12.5 cm.
20 in. = 50 cm.
25 in. = 62.5 cm.
42 in. = 105 cm.
45 in. = 112.5 cm.

Giving a child a picture or model to copy or adding to his painting makes him dissatisfied with his work and unsure of his ability. Avoid questions and statements such as, "What did you paint?...Do people have purple hair?...Grass is green, not pink!...This is how to make a rabbit." Such comments show that the teacher does not value or understand the child's work. Such comments also make the child feel his work is unacceptable to the teacher. Accept a child's work as an expression of his thoughts and ideas. Encourage him with positive comments, such as, "You have pretty bright colors in your picture....God made our eyes so we can see (red) and (blue) colors....Would you like to tell me about your painting?...What are you thinking about as you paint?"

Children are expected to clean up their work area when they are finished. Even a two-year-old can wipe up drips with a damp sponge or cloth.

Dry easel and finger paintings by hanging them on a small clothes-drying rack. Or, hang a fishnet or several strands of clothesline along one wall. Attach wet paintings with clothespins. Paintings become an added room decoration.

Materials for *gadget printing* include paint, paper, a variety of gadgets, paper towels and shallow containers such as foil pans. Paint and paper are the same as those used for easel painting. Gadgets can come from several sources. From the kitchen use forks, cookie cutters, a potato masher, sponges, tubes from paper towels; lemons and oranges cut in half; potatoes or carrots with a design cut in the end. Use empty spools from the sewing basket. Your gadget collection might also include erasers, pipe cleaners, corks, small plastic bottles, hair rollers, corn husks, and pieces of sponge clipped into clothespins.

Dampen and fold two or three paper towels together to form a pad slightly smaller than the container in which they will be placed. Pour paint on the pad and allow it to soak in. The child presses his gadget on the pad and then on his paper. To simplify cleaning gadgets soak them in warm, soapy water.

String painting is an interesting variation of gadget painting. Clip a clothespin to one end of a piece of string. The child dips the string in paint, then drags it across his paper. The process can be repeated several times.

Spot painting requires a muffin tin, white powdered detergent, tempera paint, plastic spoons and white construction paper. Half fill with detergent several cups in the muffin tin. Add enough tempera paint and water to make a gravy-like consistency. Place a plastic spoon in each tin. Fold pieces of paper in half. The child opens the paper and places *spots* of paint on one side. The child folds the other half on top and presses gently. When opened, a print appears.

Clay: Clay and various types of salt/flour dough are excellent manipulative materials for young children. Children enjoy helping to make dough before using. Potter's clay can be purchased in powdered form or already mixed and ready to use. (Do not confuse this material with oil base modeling clay.) Powdered clay is mixed with water until it is about the consistency of bread dough. Knead the clay to distribute the moisture evenly. Let the newly made clay age until it can be handled without sticking to hands. Clay and dough must be kept in airtight containers to prevent drying out.

The tabletop should be covered when working with clay. The reverse side of oilcloth taped to a piece of heavy cardboard makes an ideal clay board. Aprons should be worn when working with clay. Sponges are needed for cleanup.

Clay is ready to use when you can easily make a thumbprint in it. (Working with clay requires more hand strength than most twos and younger threes possess; salt/flour dough is better suited to their ability.) Give each child a piece of clay about the size of a small grapefruit. In the manipulative stage, encourage the child to push, poke, pound, pull, smash and pat the clay. This gives him ideas in how to use it. Then he may choose one or two ways to make something. Timid children may shy away from this and other "messy" activities. Never force a child to do an activity. Allow him to watch the other children, until he feels willing to try. As a child reaches the stage of making figures, he will break off bits of clay and stick them on as arms, legs, heads, ears and noses. These pieces will drop off as the clay dries. Show the child how appendages can be made by gently squeezing, pulling or "stroking" the clay. Fours and fives also enjoy using rolling pins and Popsicle sticks to roll and cut clay. Use cookie cutters with salt/flour dough.

Each child should help clean his area work and tools with a damp sponge. A dustpan and brush are needed to clean up dry crumbs of clay. Before returning the clay to its airtight container, ask the child to roll the clay into a ball. Poke a hole in the ball and fill the hole with water. This will help keep the clay pliable. As much clay as possible should be removed from tools and hands before they are washed in the sink. Clay settles along the bottom of pipes and will clog plumbing.

Cut and Paste: For cut and paste activities, provide scissors, paper and paste. Scissors should be about four inches long with blunt points. Be sure they cut easily to avoid frustrating children who are just learning to use them. Provide three or four pairs of left-handed scissors.

Cut and paste is probably best suited for older threes, fours and fives. The use of scissors depends upon the development of the small hand and arm muscles. Threes and even some fours are not ready to use scissors. They enjoy tearing the paper rather than cutting it. Twos enjoy pasting precut pieces.

Paste should be put in small containers for the child's convenience. Use Popsicle sticks or Q-tips to apply the paste. But fingers are fun, too. The child can apply the paste to the large background paper, then press the smaller piece onto that spot. White glue and glue sticks can also be used.

Children need freedom to experiment with cut and paste activities just as they do with other art materials. At first the child seems to pile the cut pieces of paper on top of each other using big lumps of paste to stick them together. He may press the lump of paste against the paper, making no attempt at smoothing it. Later he may paste the pieces he has cut so they extend over the edge of his background paper. Refrain from changing the child's work or suggesting where he paste his cut pieces. But don't be afraid to guide the amount of paste used!

For five-year-olds, cut and paste can evolve into a *tissue lamination* project. Provide tissue paper in two or three different colors for this activity. A piece of card stock or heavy paper can be used as a background. The child "paints" the background paper with liquid starch or diluted white glue. A wide paint brush (two or three inches wide) will do this job quickly. Next, he cuts or tears colored tissue paper into various sizes and shapes and lays them on the paper. The child completes his picture by brushing over the tissue paper with a small amount of starch or glue. If the tissue gets too wet, the colors may run. Tissue may also be glued on other material such as cottage cheese containers, and cardboard tubes. Sometimes tissue paper is hard for even five-year-olds to cut. Be sure to have extra precut pieces available.

Children should be encouraged to put paper scraps back in the box when finished. A damp sponge is needed to wipe paste off the tables and fingers. Sort through the scrap paper box periodically to remove any faded or soiled construction paper.

Collage: Materials for collage can be as varied as your imagination. Include pieces of fabric, lace, paper, buttons, rickrack, string, carpeting, macaroni, straws, cotton, beads, burlap or string bags, foil, yarn, colored rice, beans and peas. From outdoors gather feathers, dried weeds, seeds and seed pods, twigs, seashells, leaves, lichen, sand or gravel.

The child will need white glue or paste and a piece of heavy paper or lightweight cardboard (approximately 12″x18″—30 x 45 cm) on which to glue his materials. Cardboard makes a good background since some materials are too heavy for paper. Scissors will be needed to cut some of the materials.

Making a collage stimulates a child's imagination and adds to his sense of achievement. Any combination of materials can be interesting. This is an activity at which every child can succeed because there is no right or wrong way to assemble a collage. Let the child enjoy experimenting with the materials. Avoid comparing one child's work with that of another.

Place collage materials in one or two shallow boxes or cake pans so a child can easily see and reach them. Select items that have some relationship to each other; for a creation lesson, use a variety of leaves; another time have things mommy sews with (yarn, buttons, material scraps). Making choices from too wide a selection is confusing, causing children to lose interest. Occasionally use backgrounds other than sheets of paper: paper plates and cups, fabric pieces, or large, empty cans.

Drawing/Coloring: For coloring activities provide large sheets (12″x18″ [30x45 cm]) of paper (Newsprint, butcher paper, shelf paper or the reverse side of wallpaper or wrapping paper) and large crayons.

Large or jumbo crayons about four inches long and ⅜-inch in diameter, are easily held by young children. Some crayons should have the paper removed so the child can use the sides of the crayon. Periodically sort out and discard short, unusable crayons.

The young child is capable of expressing himself through his own marks or pictures. He does not need outlines such as found in coloring books. These predetermined shapes set a standard the child cannot reach, undermining his creative development and his self-confidence. The child becomes dissatisfied with his own efforts. The young child's small muscle development does not allow him to color within the lines as expected in coloring books.

Crayon resist is done by brushing watercolors or thin tempera over a crayon drawing. The water runs off the wax crayon and the design or drawing stands out.

Four and fives enjoy crayon rubbings. Gather objects such as leaves, coins or pieces of varying textured fabric. Place an object under a large sheet of thin paper. The child rubs the side of a crayon over the object, holding the paper still with his other hand. The outline and texture of the object appear on the paper.

Bible Teaching/Learning Opportunities ■ NOTE: Young children tend to concentrate fiercely while working on some art projects. In such cases, conversation is best saved for after they are finished.

Sharing/Kindness: Because most Early Childhood art projects are individual efforts, not group projects, teachers must plan carefully to create situations in which children interact with each other. One effective approach is to call attention to the necessity for the children to share materials and wait turns. As children work, identify specific acts of cooperative behavior. "Stacey is sharing her sponge with Mark. Our Bible tells us to 'share with others....' You are a kind helper, Brad. Thank you for picking up those spilled crayons....Thank you for clipping Cheryl's paper on the easel, Greg. Our Bible tells us to help each other....Jack, you may put the brushes in the water to soak. Mary may throw the newspapers away. I will put the paint on the sink. When we help each other we clean up very quickly."

Extend the child's learning by writing on his paper an account of a way he was kind, or a Bible thought you discussed with him.

Bible Thoughts for your conversation: "Help each other," Proverbs 12:12 (*TLB*); "Share with others," 1 Timothy 6:18 (*TLB*).

Creation: Collages using nature items are easy for conversation about creation: "You have a seed pod on your collage, Betsy. God planned for seeds to grow in seed pods. The seeds blew away. Now the pod is empty. It's what you need for your collage...." Other activities call for focusing on the God-given skills the child is using in doing the project.

"God made your hands just right for finger painting, Charles. It is God who has made us.... Clay is a special kind of dirt. God made the dirt. All things were made by God."

While three children finger-painted, Mr. Dunn sang softly, "Jenny has hands that can paint, paint, paint. Don has hands that can paint, paint, paint! Lee has hands that will paint, paint, paint! God has made our hands!"

Bible Thoughts for your conversation:

"God made the world and everything in it." (See Acts 17:24.)

"There is nothing too hard for God." (See Jer. 32:17.)

"It is God who has made us." Psalm 100:3

Storytelling

Storytelling can take place anytime during the morning, but especially during Bible Story Time (Sunday School) and Tell-Me-Time (Church Time).

Storytelling, a teaching method centuries old, has many values for the young child. It helps the child learn to listen and thus increases his attention span. Listening to stories helps develop the child's ability to retain a sequence of ideas. It gives him experience in speaking and helps increase his vocabulary as he talks about stories he has heard. Storytelling is most valuable for young children when it reinforces and coincides with firsthand experiences from the child's life.

One purpose of storytelling in the Sunday School is to share the gospel of God's love and the effect of this love on his own life. Therefore, we tell Bible stories that are within his interest and that reflect a bit of his own everyday experiences. The world of a young child involves experiences with his home, family, a few animals, nature, church, and modes of travel. Bible stories must be based on some part of this experience in order to begin with something he knows.

In addition to stories from the Bible, present-day stories are an effective teaching tool for communicating Scripture truths to young children. Children respond to stories about children their own age who do things they enjoy. These stories should always reinforce the basic truth of the Bible story told that morning.

The attention span of many toddlers and two-year-olds does not enable them to sit with a group to listen to a story. Therefore, briefly tell the Bible story many times throughout the morning whenever one or more children show an interest. Even when twos can participate in group experiences this practice should continue. Young children need—and like—to hear the story again and again. Remember that for toddlers and twos the "story" does not require much action or plot. A clear account of a simple event is all that is required. Give them just one idea and one person to identify.

A three-year-old's attention span allows him to listen to stories up to about three minutes long. Fours and fives can listen up to five minutes.

Fours and fives are interested in the action of a story—the "what" and the "how." The names of people and places, the dates of events (the "where," "who" and "when") have little meaning to young children.

Materials ■ The most important piece of equipment needed for Bible storytelling is your Bible! Keep it open so the children recognize it as the source of your story. Your *Teacher's Manual* is also important, but use it for study during the week, not on Sunday morning. Visual resources such as pictures, Bible story figures and puppets can be used to visualize a story. These resources reinforce and give meaning to your words. For a child who has never seen a sheep or a well, pictures are essential to his learning.

Procedure ■ Begin your story preparation early in the week. Read the story from the Bible. Read it again from a modern translation. Avoid the temptation to skip reading the story in the Bible "because I know it so well."

Next, read the story in your *Teacher's Manual*. This will help you tell the story in words the child will understand. It is also a guide for the use of specific visual resources. Notice the teaching/learning aim printed at the beginning of the lesson. This indicates the major emphasis the curriculum writers have taken in preparing the story.

Several times during the week practice telling the story and using the visual resources. You may find it helpful to make an outline on a small card to put in your Bible. Know the story well enough so you can look directly at the children most of the time.

During the Bible Learning Activities, look for opportunities to say something like, "What you just did reminds me of a Bible story. Would you like to hear a story?" If the child is interested, tell him the story then. There is no need to fear reducing interest during Bible Story Time. Young children like stories best when they are familiar.

At Bible Story Time, see that the children are seated comfortably and can easily see any visuals you are using. Be sure distractions, such as toys, books or purses are out of sight. To help children get ready to listen, catch their attention with a finger fun or simple action song. Each time before you teach remind them that the story you are about to tell them is true—it really happened to some real people a long time ago. It is from the Bible and everything in the Bible is true and important for us to hear and learn.

Introduce the story by reminding children of something they have done that morning that was similar to some action in the story.

Tell the story in your normal voice. Let your genuine interest in the story come through. Also speak clearly, distinctly and slowly. Create excitement by speaking slightly faster. Whisper or pause briefly to create suspense. "The shepherds hurried down the streets of Bethlehem. Faster and faster they walked. When they came to the stable they went inside. They saw Mary and Joseph. And in the manger they saw (pause) the baby Jesus!"

To keep children's interest use repetition and action verbs. "Peter's friends helped him pull in the heavy nets of fish. Pull...pull...pull. They used their strong arms to pull the nets." You pretend to pull the net as you talk! Put yourself in the place of each character and speak and act as they would. Bend over slightly and put a shawl over your shoulders as you tell the story of the widow who gave all she had. Facial expressions convey many feelings. Look angry or frightened. Smile a big smile. The children will often respond with the same expression on their faces!

Asking questions during the story may secure participation, but can also cause some children to lose track of the narrative. For the same reason, avoid letting children use the story visuals. Keep the story moving to retain interest.

When the story ends, use your closing sentence and stop! In order to keep your listening period within the child's attention span, avoid lengthy applications and comments. The main point should have been clearly made during the story. All that is needed are a few simple questions to check on children's understanding, then present the Bible Thought to introduce the Activity page.

The Bible story should be reviewed during Church Time. Fours and fives will enjoy helping to retell it, possibly using the visuals themselves once they are familiar with the story details.

Bible Teaching/Learning Opportunities ▪ Your Bible story should obviously be chosen to fit the Bible teaching/learning aim of your lesson.

Sharing/Kindness or Helping: Your story might be "Feeding the Five Thousand," "The Woman at the Well" or "Jesus Stilling the Storm." If your aim involves Creation your story could be a portion from Genesis. If your aim involves *Thankfulness*, your story might be one that illustrates God's loving care, such as Jacob's dream. The wise teacher will use these stories, not just for their own sake as interesting stories, but to illustrate simple concepts the child needs to understand.

Music

Use singing throughout the entire Sunday School and Church Time program. Use listening activities most often during Bible Learning Activities (Sunday School) and Choosing Time (Church Time).

Of all the words spoken in your department on Sunday morning, the ones children will remember the longest are the ones set to music. Melody and rhythm give words great impact, making them easy to remember and repeat. Thus, music is one of a teacher's most powerful tools and should be carefully planned to support Bible teaching/learning aims. Songs should be chosen because they clearly and simply say what the child should remember after the session. Symbolic songs have no place in Early Childhood.

Music is a natural expression of feelings and experiences. When a child feels secure and relaxed, he will often sing or hum spontaneously as he plays. Through music a shy child can become involved in group activity; an overstimulated child can be helped to relax; an overactive, aggressive child can release his tensions in an acceptable way.

Observe a group of children involved in play and you will notice that they make up their own songs, chants and games as they play. They respond to the rhythm of a swing, a jump rope or the wind. Music is an outlet for this creativity and a means of self-expression. With the aid of music a child can become a horse or a butterfly, an elephant or a clown. He can use his hands, his feet or his whole body to express how the music makes him feel. Through music he can work off his energy and stretch large muscles in acceptable ways.

Music can help children get acquainted and establish friendly feelings. Simple musical games using the child's name can help the child feel accepted. As the children gathered together for group time, Mrs. Martin began to sing, "Here we are together....There's Karen and Tommy and Peter and Robin...." Hearing his own name helped each child feel an important part of the group.

Music provides the child with opportunities to respond to God in thankfulness and love. As the children looked at a snowflake through a magnifying glass, Mrs. Thomas softly sang, "Thank you, God, I thank you, God. Thank you, God, for snowflakes."*

A child under three will usually just watch and listen as you sing. When he has heard a song several times a two-year-old may begin to respond by singing an occasional word or phrase with you. When the song includes actions he will often respond with a few of the motions. He enjoys hearing the same songs again and again.

The three-year-old is beginning to sing with the teacher, though he may be a few words behind. He enjoys singing familiar songs and will often ask, "Sing it again." Threes enjoy action songs and simple rhythm activities, even though they cannot yet keep time accurately.

Fours and fives enjoy singing with other children. They like using simple rhythm instruments. Fours and fives can make their own simple songs about what they've seen or done. Most fives have the ability to sing words and do motions at the same time.

There is no "song service" in a department for young children. Rather, music is used naturally and informally to help children learn specific Bible truths.

---

*Note: All songs referred to in this book are from the songbook *Little Ones Sing*. They have been carefully selected to help young children learn basic Bible truths. The thoughtful teacher will learn and use these songs consistently as he presents God's Word in a variety of interesting and meaningful ways.

Materials ■ You already possess the most important piece of basic equipment—your voice. Add to that a knowledge of songs appropriate to your Bible teaching/learning aims, and you are ready to use music. Remember that your interest, enthusiasm and your familiarity with the songs are far more important than a professionally trained voice.

Songs for the young child should be short, rhythmic and tuneful. The words should be related to the child's interests and experiences. The teacher needs to have many songs ready at a moment's notice.

All departments for young children need a sturdy, easy-to-operate record player and a selection of activity records and listening records. Increasingly popular are record players equipped with earphone jacks enabling several children to listen to a record without disturbing others.

Rhythm instruments are an important musical tool. Rhythm instruments can be purchased or made. They should include drums, wood blocks, bells, rhythm sticks, tambourines and shakers. Five-year-olds can make some of these rhythm instruments as a Bible learning activity.

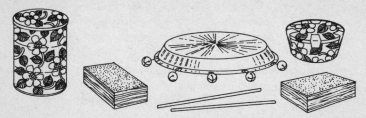

Sandpaper Blocks: Use two sanded blocks of wood about 6"x3" (15x7.5 cm) for each set of blocks. Firmly glue coarse sandpaper on face of each block.

Tambourines: Punch holes around side of a heavy-duty aluminum foil plate. Push loop of Christmas bell or baby rattle bell through each hole and fasten on inside with a small safety pin as shown.

Shakers: Place a handful of rice or dry beans in empty ice-cream, cottage cheese or sour cream carton. Glue lids securely or seal with heavy gummed tape. Decorate with pieces of colored gummed paper.

Drum: Use coffee can with plastic lid. Decorate with piece of colored gummed paper.

Rhythm sticks: cut ¼" (.625 cm) doweling into 12" (30. cm) pieces. Allow children to sand smooth. Paint with enamel paint.

Instrumental accompaniment is not necessary with young children, except to keep the teacher on pitch. You may want to consider an autoharp. This simple stringed instrument can be mastered easily by anyone, regardless of musical ability. It is superior to a piano for accompanying young children's singing because its light tones do not overpower their small voices. Its compact size makes it adaptable for use, not only with a large group, but also in small group activities. Five-year-old children enjoy learning to play the autoharp themselves. Even twos like to strum it while a teacher plays the chords.

Procedure ■ Babies especially enjoy being sung to. Teachers can sing simple songs while rocking, feeding or changing a child. A lullaby is an age-old tool for helping babies sleep.

At activity centers, teachers should be ready with songs related to the lesson aim. As the children plant seeds, the teacher might sing softly, "Who made the seeds? God did...." While children work with collage materials, the teacher might comment that the children are using the hands God made for them; then sing, "Thank you, God. I thank you, God. Thank you, God, for my hands."

Music can be used during Bible Story Time to relate a Bible story truth to the child's everyday experience. For example, at the conclusion of the story about Jesus calling His helpers, the teacher used the Bible verse, "Come, learn of me." As the children completed invitations asking friends to Sunday School, the teacher sang, "Come, learn of Me. Come, learn of Me. Come, learn of Me, Jesus said."

During Together Time, children and teachers sing to reinforce learning experiences shared during Bible Learning Activities. In a lesson focused on responding thankfully for God's love, the leader might say, "I saw some children in the Home Living corner who were praying. They were thanking God for loving them. That made me want to sing a song about being thankful." The group then sang, "Be Thankful Unto Him."

When children become restless or inattentive the wise teacher sings an activity song that allows the children to stretch and move tired muscles. Mrs. Black knew the children needed a change from quiet listening. So she began singing, "Let me show you how I clap hands..." The children began to sing with her. They sang the song several times using a variety of actions, such as stretching high, hopping and bending low. The concluding verse "Let me show you how I sit tall..."—helped the children get ready for the next activity.

To introduce a new song use pictures or objects to illustrate the words. Let the children hear you sing the song several times before you ask them to sing it with you. Suggest that five-year-olds listen for a certain word or phrase as you sing. Never ask children to "sing as loud as you can."

A song will catch the attention of children more quickly than a spoken command. Announce cleanup with a song, such as "Time to put away your blocks, trucks and dolls and all your toys..." While children put away materials the teacher might sing "I can help pick up my toys...."

Listening to records helps children relax during Rest Time. Interesting pictures may result when instrumental music is played while children finger paint or paint at easels. Babies and toddlers enjoy soft background music during their session.

Bible Teaching/Learning Opportunities

Creation: As children observe the wonders of God revealed in nature, music can enrich this learning experience. The children went for a walk on a warm spring day. They stopped to look at the blossoming trees and listen to the singing birds. As they looked and listened, the teacher sang, "God made our wonderful world..."

As twos and threes watched fish in the aquarium, the teacher sang, "Who made the fish? God did...."

Bible Thoughts for your conversation:

"God loves you." (See John 16:27.)

"All things were made by God." (See John 1:3.)

"God made the world and everything in it." (See Acts 17:24.)

Prayer: Music is a natural way for children to pray to God. A child may want to do so several times throughout the morning. Prayers are not limited to a specific time in the schedule. Children arranging a bouquet of spring flowers might sing. "Thank you, God. I thank you, God. Thank you, God, for pretty flowers."

The children were finger painting. Mr. Anderson said, "I'm glad God loves us and watches us. He's even interested in Brian's blue painting." As the children worked, Mr. Anderson sang, "God is very near."

Bible Thoughts for your conversation:

"It is good to give thanks to the Lord." Psalm 92:1

"I will pray to the Lord for you." 1 Samuel 7:5

"We know that God hears us." (See 1 John 5:15.)

BASIC FURNISHINGS AND EQUIPMENT FOR BABIES AND TODDLERS

■ Babies

Quiet Experiences

Books/Pictures | Picture books of fabric or cardboard (washable) · Pictures mounted on cardboard, covered with clear adhesive paper

God's Wonders | Nature materials (cut flowers, plants, fish) · Unbreakable mirror

Music | Record player/Cassette player · Assortment of recordings (lullabies, simple songs)

Feeding/Rest/Changing | Bottle warmer · Refrigerator · Baby schedule card · Changing table or carts · Disposable diapers · Soft paper towels, tissues, cotton balls · Baby oil · Sterilizing solution · Blankets, sheets

Active Experiences

Dolls | Dolls with rubber molded heads · Washable squeeze toys · Washable cuddle toys

Toys | Rattles · Crib mobile · Balls (5" to 9"—12.5x22.5 cm diameter) · Washable fabric blocks · Baby exerciser · Clutch ball · Texture ball

General Equipment

Cribs (hospital type) · Playpen (nylon mesh) · Blankets, sheets · Safety chair · Adult rocker (2) · Wall supply cabinets · Plastic wastebasket · Adult coatrack · Toilet and sink

■ Toddlers

Quiet Experiences

Books/Pictures | Picture books of fabric or cardboard (washable) · Pictures mounted on cardboard, covered with clear adhesive paper

God's Wonders | Nature materials (cut flowers, plants, fish, small animals) Magnifying glass · Unbreakable mirror

Music | Record player/cassette player · Assortment of recordings activity songs, lullabies, (simple songs)

Feeding/Rest/Changing | Paper cups, napkins · Changing table · Disposable diapers · Soft paper towels, tissues, cotton balls · Baby oil · Sterilizing solution · Blankets, sheets

Active Experiences

Dolls | Dolls with plastic molded heads · Washable squeeze toys · Washable cuddle toys · Doll bed (28"x14"x11"—70x35x27.5 cm) · Doll blankets · Plastic telephones · Soft plastic dishes · Small round table (optional)

Toys | Push and pull toys · Fill and dump toys · Nesting and stacking puzzles · Wooden jigsaw puzzles (3-4 pieces) · Large cardboard blocks · Balls (5"—9" 12.5 to 22.5 cm diameter) · Open shelf for storage · Rocking boat/Climbing steps · Ride on toys

General Equipment

Adult rocker · Wall supply cabinets · Plastic wastebasket · Coatracks (adult and child) · Toilet and sink

---

BASIC FURNISHINGS AND EQUIPMENT FOR 2s and 3s

Activity Areas	Furniture	Equipment and Materials
Home Living	Cabinet sink unit (24"—60 cm high work surface) Stove (24"—60 cm high) Table (30"x48"—75 x 120 cm surface or round w/40"—100 cm diameter, 20"—50 cm high) 4-6 chairs (10"—25 cm high) Doll bed (28"x14"x11"—70x35x27.5 cm) Rocking chair, child-sized Ironing board	Bible with pictures Safe plastic dishes Doctor play materials Dolls, rubber molded head Dress-up clothes (male & female) Two plastic telephones Doll bedding Bible with pictures
Art	Painting easel (2-sided) Table (30"x48"—75x120 cm surface 20"—50 cm high) 4-6 chairs (10"—25 cm high) Small clothes drying rack (for wet paintings) Open shelves with closed back (12"—30 cm deep)	Long-handled paintbrushes, ¾" bristles Paste Large newsprint sheets Salt/flour dough or Play-Doh Tempera, assorted colors Smocks or aprons Large crayons Sponges

Books	Book rack (27"—67.5 cm high)	Bible with pictures Books recommended in Teacher's Manual
God's Wonders	Low, open shelves with closed back (12"—30 cm deep)	Bible with pictures Nature materials (plants, aquarium, magnifying glass)
Blocks	Open shelves with closed back (12"—30 cm deep) Balance beam (4" to 6"—10 to 15 cm wide)	Bible with pictures Blocks (large cardboard for twos, wooden for threes) Sturdy wooden trucks, cars, etc. Block accessories (people, animals, etc.) Balls (7" to 9"—17.5 to 22.5 cm diameter)
Puzzles	Puzzle rack Table (30"x48"—75x120 cm) sur- face or round w/40"—100 cm diameter, (20"—50 cm high) 4-6 chairs (10"—25 cm high)	Bible with pictures Wooden puzzles (3-12 pieces) Gadget board Large wooden beads Felt boards
Music/Worship	Record player/Cassette player Autoharp	Bible with pictures Pictures as recommended in Teacher's Manual Recordings listed in Teacher's Manual *Little One Sing* songbook
Miscellaneous	2 wall supply cabinets (50"—125 cm from floor) Coatracks for adults and children Secretary's desk Toilets Sink or plastic dishpans	Record forms Sterilizing solution Plastic wastebasket

---

BASIC FURNISHINGS AND EQUIPMENT FOR 4s and 5s

Activity Areas	Furniture	Equipment and Materials
Home Living	Cabinet sink unit (24"—60 cm high work surface) Stove (24"—60 cm high) Table (30"x48"—75x120 cm surface or round w/40"—100 cm diameter, 22"—55 cm high) 4-6 chairs (12"—30 cm high) Doll bed (28"x14"x11"—70x35x27.5 cm) Rocking chair, child-sized Chest of drawers (24"—60 cm high) Ironing board	Bible with pictures Soft plastic dishes Doctor play materials Dolls (10" to 20"—25 to 50 cm long) Two plastic telephones Cleaning materials, child-sized (mop, broom, dustpan) Cooking utensils, child-sized Doll bedding Dress-up clothes (male & female)
Art	Painting easel (2-sided) Table (30"x48"—75x120 cm surface or round w/40"—100 cm diameter, 22"—55 cm high) 4-6 chairs (12"—30 cm high) Small clothes drying rack Open shelves with closed back (12"—30 cm deep)	Bible with pictures Long-handled brushes, ¾"—1.9 cm bristles Construction paper Large crayons Finger paints Manila paper, large sheets Newsprint, large sheets Smocks Paste, white glue, glue sticks Salt/flour dough or clay Tempera, assorted colors Scissors (blunt tip)
Books	Book rack (33"—82.5 cm high) Table (30"x48"—75x120 cm surface or round w/40"—100 cm diameter, 22"—55 cm high) 4 chairs (12"—30 cm high)	Bible with pictures Books recommended in Teacher's Manual
God's Wonders	Low open shelves with closed back (12"—30 cm deep)	Bible with pictures Nature materials (plants, aquarium, magnifying glass, magnet, etc.)

Blocks	Open shelves with closed back (12"—30 cm deep)	Bible with pictures Sturdy wooden trucks, cars, etc. Blocks (wooden unit) Block accessories (people, animals, etc.)
Puzzle	Puzzle rack Table (24"x36"—60x90 cm surface or round w/40"—100 cm diameter, 22"—55 cm high)	Bible with pictures Wooden puzzles (10+ pieces) Gadget board Felt boards
Music/Worship	Record player/Cassette player Autoharp	Bible with pictures Rhythm instruments Recordings, as recommended in Teacher's Manual *Little Ones Sing* songbook
Miscellaneous	2 wall supply cabinets (50"—125 cm from floor) Bulletin boards (child's eye level) Coatracks Secretary's desk Toilets Sink or plastic dishpans	Record forms Plastic wastebasket

Learning to Schedule for Children

SUNDAY MORNING SCHEDULE

The Sunday morning schedule for Early Childhood is different from any other department in the church. This is because the children in Early Childhood are different from any other people in the church.

How Do I Schedule the Time?

The stated time your church has announced for Sunday School has no significance to small children. Sunday School begins the moment the first child steps inside the door. His entrance into the room seems to shout, "Ready or not, here I come!"

This means the teachers had better be ready! Thus, Sunday School begins for the staff at least 15 minutes before the first child arrives. It is imperative that the first few minutes of each child's morning in your room be marked by warm, personal attention from a teacher. You won't be able to provide this essential touch unless you have done all your preparing and organizing ahead of time.

What is the scene in your room when the first child appears at the door? It should look like this: All equipment and materials in place where children can see them and reach them easily; the Department Leader at the door, ready to welcome each child personally; each teacher in an activity area, prepared to help children learn; (the number of activities a department can offer at one time is determined by the number of teachers); the secretary with the record materials in order and ready to assist the leader in greeting children.

Here comes the first child. The leader bends down to welcome him by name. "Charles, I'm so glad to see you. We have lots of things for you to do today!" While talking with the child, the leader makes a quick observation of the child's health status. Any signs of fever or cold warrant not admitting the child in order to protect the other children. After a friendly but brief word to the parents Charles is brought into the room.

He may need a bit of help with his coat. However, the leader wisely lets the child do as much for himself as possible. Charles finds his own name tag (he's four). Next he visits the Love Gift Center where the leader says, "We bring our love gifts because we love God." Charles is now ready to choose the activity he wants to explore first. The leader makes suggestions only when needed, but no effort is made to force a child to participate against his will.

As the other children arrive the same procedure continues. Teachers remain at their assigned areas whether or not children have begun working at that activity. The leader does seek to guide children to the less crowded areas.

If Charles were under two years old the procedures would be much the same. The parents would check his file card to see if eating and sleeping information is still current. The leader would check to be sure the diaper bag is properly marked and stored. Then Charles would begin his morning with a favorite toy—either in a crib, a playpen or on the floor, depending on his age. The rest of the morning for a baby or toddler involves individual interaction with teachers in play, conversation, singing, feeding and resting.

SUNDAY MORNING FOR BABIES AND TODDLERS

▪ Babies

Welcome

☐ Speak warmly and softly to each baby.
☐ Place baby in crib with toy.
☐ Have parents complete feeding/sleeping schedule card or check card on file.
☐ Have parents label all personal belongings (if not already done).
☐ Attach identification tags to diaper bag; put in designated place.
☐ Be alert for symptoms of illness. Do not admit baby with signs of cold or other sickness.
☐ Keep parents and older children outside room.

During Session

☐ Follow instructions on each baby's feeding/sleeping schedule card.
☐ Talk and sing softly to babies while feeding and diapering.
☐ Wash hands thoroughly after diapering each baby.
☐ Cuddle and rock each baby; play gently.
☐ Provide one or two changes of toys for each baby.
☐ Show book and/or picture; talk about each item.
☐ Show God's Wonders items; talk about each one.
☐ Resterilize all toys after use.
☐ Keep each baby's belongings in designated place.
☐ Cuddle and rock crying babies.

Departure

☐ Release baby only to parents or other adult designated by parents.
☐ Describe baby's morning to parents, especially any deviations from schedule.
☐ Have parents double check baby's belongings.
☐ File feeding/sleeping card.
☐ Remove sheets from cribs.
☐ Wash toys and put away.
☐ Leave room in order.

▪ Toddlers

Welcome

☐ Speak warmly and softly to each child, stooping to child's eye level.
☐ Help child get involved with learning materials or with another teacher. Comfort if crying.

☐ Have parents label all personal belongings if not already done.
☐ Attach identification tag to diaper bag; put in designated place.
☐ Be alert for symptoms of illness. Do not admit child showing signs of cold or other sickness.
☐ Keep parents and older children outside room.

During Session

☐ Talk and sing softly to children in all activities.
☐ Play gently and lovingly with each child; cuddle child when he desires.
☐ Provide duplicate toy in case of conflict.
☐ Show books and pictures; talk about each item.
☐ Show God's Wonders items; talk about each one.
☐ Participate with child in doll play.
☐ Help as needed in working puzzles.
☐ Assist with use of rocking boat/climbing steps.
☐ Participate in block building.
☐ Talk lovingly while changing diaper. Wash hands.
☐ Comfort crying child; provide favorite activity.

Departure

☐ Release child only to parents or other adult designated by parents.
☐ Describe child's morning to parents; specifically recount positive achievements.
☐ Have parents double check child's belongings.
☐ Wash toys thoroughly and put away.
☐ Leave room in order.

Bible Learning Activities ■ Why begin with a choice of activities? There are several reasons. First, children do not all arrive at the same time. If the session began with large group time, the constant interruption of children arriving would greatly distract the group's attention.

Second, few children come to Sunday School mentally and physically ready to sit quietly. It's too early in the day for that. They are filled with energy and vitality; they want something to do! Bible Learning Activities provide a purposeful and acceptable means of releasing this energy.

Third, the activities that teachers provide are prepared to capture children's interest and to naturally guide their thinking to the learning objective for the day. As the child begins playing with clay, the teacher at that table may say, "The clay feels good, doesn't it? The Bible says that God gives us all good things."

Fourth, even young children prefer to make their own choices. A multitude of discipline problems can be avoided by allowing a child to select from among several possibilities, rather than telling him he must do what everyone else is doing. Giving a child a choice helps him learn to make decisions and to accept responsibility. It also shows that you have respect for him.

Throughout Bible Learning Activity time, children are allowed to move freely to whatever activity they desire. When they tire of one activity, they move to another. This freedom of movement creates a relaxed atmosphere that both teachers and children enjoy. In order to keep the flow of children smooth and pleasant, the leader needs to be free in the room to guide the children into new activities by suggesting one or two alternatives. He might say, "Johnny, if you're tired of building with blocks, you could walk over to the art table to see what's happening there."

Some observers ask, "When do the children stop playing and start learning?" Play is the way God planned for small children to do most of their learning. As a child engages in building with blocks, painting at the easel, living out real experiences in the Home Living area, he is learning how to relate to other children. He is discovering that church is a place of true concern about the important things in his life. As a teacher casually asks questions and engages the child in conversation, the child is led to begin thinking about the lesson concepts for that morning. And often there is opportunity to spontaneously share a Bible Thought, to sing a song or tell the Bible story. Because this firsthand learning is so important to young children, at least half of the Sunday School session is spent in these activities.

During this time of small group activities the Department Leader moves from group to group, quietly assisting where needed. Behavior problems, such as crying children, can be handled by the leader, thus allowing teachers to focus on the group in their area. The leader is also able to observe each teacher at work, which is essential for the leader to be able to encourage teachers in specific ways to improve.

Bible Learning Activity time concludes when the leader indicates with a musical signal on the autoharp, by starting a song or by flicking the lights that it is time to clean up. Children learn responsibility and the importance of helping when they participate in cleanup. Cleanup tasks also help develop the child's sense of accomplishment as well as fostering respect and pride in his room. Open shelves that are easily accessible make cleanup easy and pleasant for the children. The children come to the circle as they complete cleanup tasks. The leader is already at the circle leading activity songs or finger fun as the children join him.

An Early Childhood department provides a variety of simultaneous activities from which each child is free to choose.

Together Time ■ The second major time block in the schedule brings all the children and teachers together in a semicircle on the rug.

There are several reasons for having a large group time. First, it helps the leader develop and express a group feeling of unity and concern. Children lift their eyes beyond their own interests and begin to see themselves as part of a larger group where they are both important and responsible. Assume that children will join. Identify children who are responding positively. Other children will be drawn by this attention.

Simple games and songs help children become aware of each other. When leader begins to sing "I have a good friend, _____ is his name," attention is focused on individual children and teachers in the group. By asking the group, "Who is not here today?" or leading them in prayer for a child who is ill, the leader is building a concern for others.

The large group also allows participation in activities that might be disruptive if done by only a few. Singing, marching, and finger play may be done in small groups, but when everyone is participating there is no worry about disturbing those involved in another activity.

Bringing everyone together provides opportunities for the leader to reinforce the Bible learning that took place during Bible Learning Activities. Conversation, songs, finger fun, an activity or prayer, all serve to call attention to the lesson focus.

The large group experience gives the Department Leader a chance for in-service teacher training. As teachers observe the leader talking with children and involving them in activities, they can improve their own teaching techniques.

Finally, the large group time changes the pace of the morning. Children will tire less readily when they are given a change of activity. Doing something new always sparks interest.

Are all young children ready for group time? By the time a child is past three, a 7-to-10-minute group time is effective for most. Two-year-olds and even some toddlers can participate in group time if it is kept very brief. They should not be required to participate in group activities. Some will participate eagerly; some will observe from the sidelines; others will ignore the group completely. Together Time should include songs and finger fun. Keep in mind the young child's need for movement and repetition. Choose songs and finer fun that allow the child to move his hands, arms and legs. Repeat familiar songs and finger fun several times rather than presenting many different ones.

Bible Story/Activity Time ■ Our objective in telling Bible stories to small children is not primarily for them to remember the details of the events. It is to allow the biblical material to speak to the child about the everyday business of living.

Bible Learning Activity time provides many opportunities to tell a Bible story. What could be more natural than during the investigation of God's Wonders for the teacher to share the story of creation? Or, when two boys in the block corner are playing well together, for a teacher to quickly tell them about David and Jonathan. Stories told informally, and applied to immediate circumstances, have by far the greatest impact. Then each retelling of the story implants its basic concept more firmly in young alert minds.

However, the realistic teacher knows that these natural opportunities to share the story will not occur every week in every activity area. Therefore, it is necessary to have a time when everyone hears the Bible story. This will be of value, both to those children who may be hearing it for the first time, and those for whom it is reinforcement of an earlier experience. This is done as the last time block of the session.

When you have more than eight or ten children, divide the children into two Bible story classes that meet with a teacher in different parts of the room. These are permanently assigned groups of no more than five to seven children. This arrangement allows children to identify closely with one particular teacher. Children need this sense of added security. With the story being told in these small groups there is ample opportunity for personal interaction between teacher and children.

These Bible story groups sit around a table or form a small circle on the floor. Each teacher presents the Bible story to his group, then leads the group in completing the activity page.

Sometimes departments find it necessary to present the Bible story to children in a large group. A shortage of teachers or an overcrowded room are reasons for doing this. The Department Leader may also use this schedule for a short time while new teachers are becoming accustomed to the children.

Departments that use this plan should divide into small class groups with individual teachers after the Bible story is told. Teachers are then able to talk about the story while leading the groups in completing their activity page, provided with the curriculum. Some groups prefer to save the activity page for the second hour, using it as one of the activity centers. Children who leave after Sunday School are given the materials to do at home.

Following completion of the activity page, one of two basic plans can be followed to insure a smooth transition to the second hour (Church Time) program. One option, which works well with fours and fives, is to have a large group song and fun time. The leader or a teacher guides children in activity songs, finger fun, exercises and simple games, as teachers oversee welcoming new arrivals or assisting those who leave.

SUNDAY SCHOOL FOR 2s THROUGH 5s

Bible Learning Activity Time	Together Time	Bible Story Activities
(Children choose from among small group and individual activities)	(Full department together for music, sharing and special features)	(Each teacher leads small group in Bible Story and activity page)
2s & 3s 40–45 min. 4s & 5s 30–35 min.	10–15 min. 15–20 min.	10–15 min. 15–20 min.
Each time sequence includes the time necessary for moving from one part of the schedule to the next.		

The second plan, which works well for all groups, is to keep the children in their small groups for transition activities, such as coloring, pegs and pegboards, working with dough, stringing beads, working puzzles, listening to music, playing the autoharp—or even having snacks. With either plan the Sunday

School staff remains involved with the children until the Church Time staff is ready to begin.

The time you have available for Sunday School must be properly utilized for best results. A plan that allows ample time for all parts of the program, and that is operated without rigidity, will insure that the best learning does take place.

Dividing the schedule into three segments gives a good change of pace to keep children from becoming restless. The length of time spent in each segment will vary according to the age level of the children.

CHURCH TIME/THE SECOND HOUR

Sunday School is just one half of most young children's morning at church. The second hour (or Church Time) is a continuation of the Sunday School's activities through the time of the church worship service. It is a vital part of the Sunday School's ministry to young children, many of whom will remain while their parents attend church. By conducting a second hour, a department doubles the time it has to communicate the teaching/learning objective for that morning. It also enables the department to communicate God's love to children whose parents come only for the worship service.

Instead of sitting through an adult service or simply being cared for in a baby-sitting program, young children can enjoy interesting learning experiences that reinforce the learning objectives taught in Sunday School. The child feels secure when the Church Time program is an extension of the Sunday School because there are no abrupt changes in procedure.

What Should Be Done During Church Time?

Church Time teachers should be aware of the teaching/learning objectives of the Sunday School so they can see the total morning experience of the child. The Church Time leader should confer regularly with the Sunday School leader to insure continuity of effort, reinforcing the learning experiences of the earlier session. The basic schedule follows the same pattern as for Sunday School.

CHURCH TIME FOR 2s THROUGH 5s

Choosing Time	Together Time	Tell-Me-Time
(Following the transition from Sunday School, children choose from Bible Learning Activities) 2s & 3s 35–40 min. 4s & 5s 30–35 min.	(Retelling of Bible Story, Snack, Rest) 15–20 min. 15–20 min.	(Aim-Related child experience story plus music and finger fun) 10–15 min. 15–20 min.
Each time sequence includes the time necessary for moving from one part of the schedule to the next.		

The second hour should include time for Bible Learning Activities, Bible story review, rest, snack, life-related story and large group activity. Bible Learning Activities should take up the first and largest block of time. As in Sunday School, these activities relate the Bible teaching/learning aim to the child's life.

A Smooth Transition from Sunday School ■ Children should remain in the same room they were in for Sunday School, with the same lesson aims. Moving them to a new room can be upsetting to some children. Since there is often the same number of children, and may even be more during the second hour, it is not a good practice to combine children from several departments during this session. Even if the group is very small, children will benefit more from close, personal attention in a room equipped for their age level.

Children and teachers may be in small group activities at the close of the Sunday School session. Older children may be enjoying song and fun time in a large group. The Department

Leader or a teacher is at the door to welcome new arrivals and to oversee the departure of those who are leaving. The door is kept closed to prevent children from leaving without an adult. Parents should wait outside the room while the leader brings their child to the door.

As each Church Time teacher arrives—as soon as possible after Sunday School—he goes directly to the Sunday School teacher he is to replace. He takes over the same activity that is in progress. Teachers who are leaving do so as quickly as possible without conversing in order to keep all disturbance to a minimum.

No attempt is made to change the activities until any transition disturbances are complete. Once things have settled down again, children return to Bible Learning Activity areas. Many teachers find they can avoid disruptive scrambles as the children move from a large group activity to activity areas by using interesting ways of moving only part of the group at once. For example, "Everyone who is wearing black shoes may stand up. Now, the ones with black shoes may find an activity you would like to do. Those with brown shoes..."

Choosing Time/Bible Learning Activities ▪ The basic pattern of allowing children to move from one activity to another is followed during the first part of Church Time just as it was during Sunday School. Again, the number of activities is based on the number of teachers, each one responsible for one area. A department with three or more teachers may repeat one or two activities from the first hour. A small department should change to new activities. For example, books could replace puzzles and blocks could replace Home Living. At least one activity area should always be new for the second hour to keep the children interested. Suggestions include preparing something to eat in the Home Living area, bringing a new plant or animal to the God's Wonders area or providing a new art experience.

When introducing the new activity be careful not to empty all the other areas. Overcrowding an activity will spoil its effectiveness. Avoid making a general announcement of a new activity. Set it up quietly. Some children will be automatically attracted to what you are doing; others will ignore it; some will be only curious spectators for a few minutes; others will become absorbed participants. Not all young children will be equally interested in any single activity. When an activity is full, instruct others who want to join that they need to find another job until there is a place to work. With a highly popular activity it may be worth keeping a sign-up chart to insure that all who desire do get a turn.

As in Sunday School, the teacher's conversation should relate the activity to the lesson's Bible teaching/learning aim. Frequently, teachers will have ideas for activities that are not in the Teacher's Manual. Accept and evaluate creative ideas in terms of your lesson aim. Avoid using activities and materials that merely entertain.

Many departments set up one center where a teacher has the Bible story visuals and involves children in retelling the Bible story. Any children who missed the first hour are guided to this center sometime during the session. Some departments also use the children's activity page as a choice at this time if it was not done during the first hour.

Spending the first part of the second hour in small groups and individual learning activities gives the teachers and children a chance to get acquainted. Emphasize the importance of being constantly alert for opportunities to weave lesson-related conversation into each activity.

If your church has a patio or outdoor play area, plan some activities for outdoors. Ten to fifteen minutes of muscle-stretching will do wonders for a small child's disposition. On a nice day a walk in the sunshine can be an enjoyable change of pace as well as a valuable learning experience. For example, children may collect nature items to make a collage. If weather or facilities do not allow going outside, another room in the building might be made available for some large muscle play.

Sometime near the beginning of the session all children should be given the chance to use the toilet. If you do not have a restroom immediately adjacent to your department, time should be set aside for each child to take care of toileting details. Two or three children can be taken together once the crowds are out of the hallways. Even with a restroom that adjoins your department, children may need to be reminded to use the toilet so they will not need to interrupt a group activity later on.

Together Time ■ When activity materials are put away children and teachers come together for singing and for Bible story review. By this time in the morning most children should know the story well, and understand the main point that is being emphasized.

Snack Time: A light, healthy snack of juice and crackers, cheese slices or fresh fruit or vegetables provides a relaxed time for conversation between teacher and children. (See "Recipes" section for more snack ideas.) This quiet time allows the teacher to become better acquainted with the children, by sitting with a small group and enjoying the snack. Children help pass napkins, share apple slices and take turns. A prayer of thanks is always a part of snack time and is most effective when done in small groups. If children have made something to eat at the Home Living area it could be served to the whole department at this time. Provision should be made for washing hands before eating. Each child is responsible for disposing of his own napkin and cup.

Rest Time: A rest time is a must during the second hour in Early Childhood departments. A few moments of quiet are essential to the well-being of active youngsters. The teachers should lie down next to the most restless children; to help them by example. A gentle touch and soft words encourage them to rest quietly. If your floor is not carpeted, mats or large towels should be provided. Darken the room slightly and play a recording of soft music. Five to ten minutes is usually ample time, but this can vary depending upon the children's need. Usually the most active children will need these moments most of all. Their restlessness is often a symptom of overstimulation or fatigue.

Tell-Me-Time ■ A large group activity follows rest time. A life-related story is told at this time. However, some children may enjoy listening to the story while resting on their mats. If so, care should be taken to be sure all children can hear the story and see the visuals. This story should relate the Bible teaching/learning aim of the morning in life experiences familiar to the child. Songs and finger fun used earlier can also be repeated here.

Concluding the Session ■ To conclude the morning, children may remain in the large group for activity songs and exercises, or, the same small group activities used between Sunday School and Church Time can be repeated. Avoid having an activity that requires extensive cleanup, so that each child can put away the materials he is using when his parents arrive. As parents arrive the leader or a teacher remains at the door and brings each child to his parents.

Whichever plan is used, it is important for children to stay involved until their parents come for them. Occasionally an insecure or exhausted child may begin to cry when he sees parents coming for other children. A teacher should reassure the child that his parents will be coming soon and try to involve him in an activity such as rocking a doll or looking at a picture book. The teacher should remain with the child until his parents arrive. A toddler or two may need the security of being held on the teacher's lap.

The leader should give each child a warm, personal good-bye. Be sure to use the child's name. Have a pleasant, positive comment for parents also. If parents wish to visit, ask them to wait until the children have left or make an appointment to talk with them during the week.

After the children leave, leader and teachers take a few minutes to be sure materials are put away and everything is in order.

While you straighten things up, talk about the session and exchange suggestions to improve next week.

SUNDAY NIGHTS

If your church wants young parents to attend the evening service, provision should be made for young children. Most children this age, at the end of a busy day, are even less capable of sitting through an adult service than they are in the morning. Establishing and maintaining a Sunday evening program for young children requires additional effort, but if your church is committed to a ministry to young families the results are well worth the work.

First, secure adequate personnel. Three basic plans are in common use. Each church should determine which will be most practical and effective in its own situation. Some develop an evening staff that functions on a regular basis in the same way as the Sunday School teachers. Some use a variation of their morning second hour program by having volunteers serve for a month at a time. Others operate with paid personnel. Paid personnel usually provide child care only. Other arrangements would have to be made to provide learning experiences for the children.

The location for your Sunday night program should be the same as for Sunday morning. Since there will probably be a considerably smaller number of young children in the evening, it may be best to combine two or more age groups. Keep in mind that it is better to have two small groups of similar age than one large group with a wider range.

When the same rooms are used in the evening as in the morning, there must be coordination between the two programs as to the use of facilities and equipment. A cooperative spirit of sharing based on mutual respect for both programs should be fostered. All groups should observe the same careful treatment of materials and equipment. A periodic meeting of the leaders of both programs is a valuable means of coordinating.

The same learning goal should be used in both evening and morning programs. Young children thrive on the familiar. The opportunity to repeat an enjoyable experience will be eagerly anticipated. If two groups of different ages have been combined, use the material designed for the younger group. Teacher's Manuals should be given to all teachers.

Activities on Sunday evening are basically the same as for the morning programs. One new activity should be added to spark interest. Planning this requires communication with the Sunday School leaders.

A sample schedule for threes through fives, based on a 75-minute program, would be:

Small Group Activities	45 minutes
Snack and Rest	15 minutes
Large Group Time	15 minutes

These time blocks would vary with the length of the service and the age of the children. Children under three would not have a large group time.

THE MIDWEEK PROGRAM

A weeknight program for birth through three years should follow the pattern for Sunday nights.

Fours and fives in many churches are provided with a choir program during this time. As a cooperative effort of the music department and education department, the objective is to develop musical skills and appreciation, not to produce a performing group. Time is spent in the regular activity areas, with music being interwoven into these learning experiences. The concepts of the songs to be sung that evening are part of the teachers' conversations in each area. Special emphasis is given to art activities related to the songs.

The large group time emphasis is on music experiences. Listening to records and various instruments, singing, humming, marching and experimenting with simple instruments should be included. Rhythm instruments are good sources of meaning-ful firsthand music experiences.

There must always be communication and coordination with other Early Childhood program leaders. It is highly important that whenever a child comes to his room he is greeted with the same loving care, and that the same behavior is expected of him. Consistent standards in all Early Childhood departments build a sense of security and confidence in young children.

Learning to Support the Home

THE INFLUENCE OF THE HOME

The properly functioning Sunday School can provide a good learning environment and loving atmosphere for small children. But young children spend most of their time at home. It is the home that really molds a child. The attitudes of parents, brothers and sisters have far greater impact on the child than do those of the Sunday School teacher who sees the child only one day a week.

Timothy grew up in a home that provided consistent Christian nurture. Both his grandmother and mother had sincere faith. They taught him the sacred writings which gave him wisdom and in turn led to his salvation. They surely must have demonstrated their teachings in their lives, for young children learn by observation and example more than be merely receiving instruction by word of mouth.

Ever since Old Testament times faithful families have been taught to be Bible-centered. This obviously implies more than "reading a chapter" together, one night a week. Parents were to weave the instruction of the Word diligently and naturally throughout all their daily activities. They were to demonstrate, and talk about, how Bible truth related to everyday life, (see Deut. 6:4-7).

The ministry of the Sunday School is incomplete when it is

disassociated from children's home. Cooperation and mutual support between Sunday School and home provide potent reinforcement and are of great value to a child's growth.

How can you, as a concerned teacher, be used to help your children's families? What can you do for the child from the non-Christian family? How can you support and encourage young parents who are looking for answers to the challenges of guiding their child? What can you offer the mature Christian parent who may have more experience and understanding than you?

In each of these situations, personal contact between teacher and parents is basic. Teachers must actively seek to get acquainted and build friendships with the parents of children assigned them. This is especially true in dealing with unchurched families. The period of life when an adult is most open to the gospel is often when there are infants or young children in the family. People who might otherwise turn a deaf ear to the gospel often become receptive because of their parental concern for their children. They sense their own inadequacies most keenly when faced with the responsibilities of molding a child's future.

All parents respond to concerned, friendly individuals who reflect God's love for their child. All teachers can benefit from the insights parents have about their own child. A teacher must approach parents, not as one who has all the answers, but as a friend who wants to support them in teaching and helping their child. In this way the teacher truly becomes "a servant," one who follows Jesus' example in offering care and concern.

CONTACT WITH PARENTS ON SUNDAYS

There are many ways to make contacts and build relationships with the families of those you teach. Your first contact with the parents, when they bring "Susie" or "Jimmy" for the first time, is of extreme importance. Personal interest in the child and his parents must be shown from the start. Having your department organized with all teachers present and activities set up at least 15 minutes before Sunday School is scheduled to start will free the Department Leader to remain at the door to greet children and parents as they arrive.

At the end of the session, also, it is important to maintain this type of organization. The teachers should remain involved with children, keeping them occupied until their parents arrive. The attitude of the child at the end of the morning speaks volumes to parents, influencing their attitudes toward the program and the teachers.

The teacher or leader who is at the door should make friendly, brief comments on each child's activities during the morning. When necessary to discuss something with the parents, arrange a convenient time for a phone call or visit that week.

Also, look for opportunities to talk briefly with parents at other times around church. Seek them out before or after services. Invite them to sit with you in church. Talk with them about matters other than their child, building gradually stronger bonds of friendship.

HOW CAN OUR DEPARTMENT COMMUNICATE WITH THE HOME?

Personal contacts of any kind help people feel important. They show that someone cares. They are means of developing mutual sharing and appreciation.

Writing

The simplest type of personal contact is a handwritten note, card or letter. Notes should be sent to both the parents and the child. Three-year-olds rarely get mail. Their excitement at receiving a card makes the effort well worthwhile. This type of contact is read at the receiver's convenience, is nonthreatening and pleasant. It shows you care and helps build good will. It is only a one-way contact, however, with no opportunity for response.

The receiver knows how you feel, but you are unaware of how the message was received.

Phoning

The telephone is also quick and easy to use and allows for conversation. It cannot embarrass anyone because of their personal appearance or the cleanliness of their home. However, the phone can interrupt, catching people at an inconvenient time. A warm voice can quickly set a person at ease and sensitive ears can let you know if you would be better off calling at another time.

Occasionally call to talk with the child. With twos and threes you may get mostly silence at the other end. But both parents and child will appreciate your interest.

Visiting

The first visit in a home should focus on explaining each phase of the Sunday School program. Describe the learning methods of the department and the basic theme and aims of the current unit you are teaching. Bring a photo album of pictures of children at work. Also show some typical samples of children's work.

Show parents the Bible story leaflets provided in the curriculum. Explain how they can use these for bedtime stories as well as for interesting activities to do with their children during the week. Some departments prefer to give parents the complete set of leaflets for the quarter. Others prefer to distribute them each Sunday after class.

An excellent follow-up is to arrange a visit just to see the child. Explain the value for a child to see you outside the classroom situation. When you come to his home, focus attention on the child rather than the adults. Visit his room and favorite toys and engage in child-level conversation. Parents will often become more open, too, as they see their child respond to the teacher's interest.

When making a home visit, observe these general guidelines:

1. Have a stated reason for calling—to deliver a gift to a sick child, explain new procedures in the department, etc.
2. Call and make an appointment to insure coming at a convenient time.
3. Make the visit with your spouse or another teacher.
4. Keep your visit brief.
5. Talk about the child's positive behavior.
6. With non-Christian parents, briefly share your relationship with Christ. Invite the parents to attend church or an adult Sunday School class. Leave a church bulletin listing activities.
7. Pray for the family concerned before and after each visit.

ORGANIZING FOR HOME CONTACTS

The most important action a department can take to enable teachers to make significant home contacts is to assign each teacher a small group of children—the same ones who are in that teacher's Bible story class.

The need to maintain personal contact with the child and his parents is one of the major reasons for maintaining teacher-child ratios no larger than one-to-six. Any teacher who is responsible for more than six children will be unable to develop and maintain close personal contact with the children and their families. It is better for a teacher to get to know a few families well than to spread the same amount of available time among more families with only superficial contact.

An important aid in keeping in touch with children's homes is an accurate system of records. These include the child's name, address, phone number and date of birth. It is helpful to include the names and ages of other family members also.

Every teacher should be aware of each child's pattern of attendance. The absence of a child on a Sunday morning should trigger a response by the teacher. Usually a phone call is the best contact after the first absence, in order to determine the reason the child was not there. Most parents appreciate a friendly inquiry, such as, "We really missed Jennie. Was anything wrong?" If the child is ill, an appropriate response can be made. To merely send cards when the reason for the absence is not known, may result in missing an opportunity to minister in a time of real need.

Absences should not be the only reason for making a contact. Otherwise, parents and children may sense they are merely objects in attendance building efforts, not people for whom teachers really care. Birthdays and special events offer good reasons to write or call, or even to invite a child out for a special treat. Keep accurate records on these contacts so that no child is overlooked.

In addition to the general Sunday School records, each teacher should keep a personal record of the progress of each child in his class. The most obvious growth appears in the areas of physical stature and ability, social interaction and vocabulary skills. Teachers also need to be aware of each child's development in relation to the basic teaching/learning objectives of the department. This evaluation could be done as part of a department planning meeting, with all the teachers contributing their observations on each child. An outline such as the one following can help guide the teachers' thinking.

EARLY CHILDHOOD PROGRESS EVALUATION

Self-Concept
1. To what extend does he become involved in activity?
2. How does he respond to new experiences?
3. How does he respond to success or failure?

Attitudes Toward Others
1. What skills does he have in participating with a group of children?
2. To what extent does he show sensitivity to the rights of others?
3. How does he respond to small groups of children? Large groups?

Attitudes Toward Church
1. What indication does he give that he likes or dislikes coming to church?
2. How does he respond toward individual teachers?
3. Is his attendance pattern improving or decreasing?

Attitude Toward Bible and Prayer
1. How does he handle the Bible?
2. How does he respond to invitation to hear a Bible story?
3. How does he respond in moments of prayer and worship?

Feelings Toward Jesus
1. What statements has he made that reflect on his understanding of Jesus?
2. What evidence does he give of having feelings that Jesus is his friend?
3. How often does he spontaneously introduce Jesus into conversation?

God Awareness
1. How does he respond in conversation about God?
2. What statements does he make that reflect his understanding of God?
3. What evidence does he give of showing awareness that God created him and the world?

Any significant indications of growth should be recorded periodically by each teacher for the children assigned to his class. Share observations with parents to secure their insight about the child's behavior at home. Interaction between teacher and parent about the child's development can be very helpful for both.

Have You Tried These Ideas?

Parents' Observation of the Department ■ During the year, invite every parent to observe at least one session in their child's department. By seeing the department in action during a full session a parent can quickly understand the objectives and teaching methods of the department. Many parents have not seen their child interacting with a group of children. Observation in a group teaching situation can provide understanding of their own child.

The parents' presence may affect a child's behavior, but by careful handling this can be minimized. Talk with the parents ahead of time and ask them to come a little early. Provide seats away from the centers of activity. Ask them to avoid talking with teachers, children, or each other, as talking will distract the children. After the parents have observed a session, discuss their response and answer any questions they may have.

Open House ■ Plan a special open house for a Sunday afternoon evening or weeknight. The children may bring their parents and participate with them in learning activities used on Sunday morning. Even toddlers enjoy getting to "play with daddy" using the department's toys. Children may help make invitations and perhaps prepare some refreshments. Provide time for parents to ask questions about the department.

Parent-Teacher Meetings ■ These meetings are usually held in the evening and may include special speakers and films. Keep the emphasis on topics that will be helpful for the parents at home: discipline, activities to enjoy with your child, family worship with preschoolers, etc. Share a list of books useful for parents. A table with books available for borrowing or purchase is helpful for parents.

Mothers' Club ■ Many churches provide regular opportunities for young mothers to meet to discuss their concerns about their children. Resource people are usually provided to keep discussion productive. Often, there is a workshop format with mothers learning various home-craft skills. In many churches the Mothers' Club is very informal and the group meets in homes. A Bible study or devotional period is usually included as part of the schedule.

Bulletin Boards and Monthly Bulletins ■ These may keep parents informed on many topics:
1. Unit goals and objectives
2. Special coming events and activities
3. Photographs of children and samples of their work
4. Activities in the church that would be of interest to parents
5. Recommended reading for parents *and* children
6. Photographs with personal information about teachers
7. A list of materials needed by the department which parents could possibly provide—for art and other activities, nature center, picture file, etc.

8. Help needed—in assistant teaching, making or repairing furniture, demonstrating a special activity.

Assistant Teaching ■ Once or twice a year, invite each parent to assist in teaching for one unit. Many churches involve parents in this way during Church Time, allowing them to work with a regular teacher. This not only gives the department added support, it gives parents opportunities to learn and practice new skills in teaching their own child. Contact the parents far enough ahead so they can schedule the time. Contact them the week before to give them instructions on what they will be doing and to share the Bible teaching/learning aims. Parents assisting may help out at one activity center; books, puzzles and God's Wonders are usually the easiest places to begin. Or parents may demonstrate a special skill that would be of interest to the children. Working together in this way gives teachers an opportunity to build rapport with the parents.

Child Visit ■ Many teachers have found an excellent response to inviting one or two children home for Sunday afternoon. The children love it. The parents appreciate it, and the teachers find it very effective in building closer relationships with each child. Many shy children have begun to open up at Sunday School following such a visit. Also, children who have been rebellious and defiant have made big strides in improved behavior. The advantages of inviting two at a time include: involving every child in class quicker, two can entertain each other, and good relationships are built among children.

YOUR COMMITMENT TO THE PARENTS

As you make personal contacts with parents, keep in mind the goal of establishing friendships and ministering spiritually to families. Become sensitive to needs they may have, including physical, material or social needs. Remember Jesus' teaching: "I was hungry, and you gave Me something to eat; I was thirsty, and you gave Me drink; I was a stranger, and you invited Me in; naked, and you clothed Me; I was sick, and you visited Me; I was in prison, and you came to Me.... To the extent that you did it to one of these brothers of Mine, even the least of them, you did it to Me" (Matt. 25:35-40). James also gives appropriate instruction: "If a brother or sister is without clothing and in need of daily food, and one of you says to them, 'Go in peace, be warmed and be filled,' and yet you do not give them what is necessary for their body, what use is that?" (Jas. 2:15,16).

You may be wondering how you are going to find time to become involved with six or seven families' lives. In order for you to have a ministry as effective as God wants it to be, teaching must be a priority in your use of time. Are there some areas in your schedule that should be dropped? Are you participating or serving in so many good causes that you cannot be truly effective in any? Make this a matter of prayerful thought to find ways of having a truly significant ministry.

Since the Bible strongly teaches that the home is the main center of teaching the Word, the teacher's ministry to the home, that of helping families to become more Christ-centered, should be as vital to him as planning the Sunday morning Bible story and learning activities.

God has given you a concern for young children. He has given you a concern for families both inside and outside the church. You have been called to minister to these homes in Jesus' name. Let Him guide you in this challenging and worthy task.

Bibliography

Arnstein, Helen. *The Roots of Love.* New York, NY: Bobbs-Merrill, 1975.

Baker, Katherine R. and Fane, Xenia F. *Understanding and Guiding Young Children.* Englewood Cliffs, NJ: Prentice-Hall, 1967.

Briggs, Dorothy. *Your Child's Self-Esteem: The Key to His Life.* Garden City, NY: Doubleday, 1970.

Chamberlain, Eugene. *When Can a Child Believe?* Nashville, TN: Broadman, 1971.

Cherry, Clare. *Creative Art for the Developing Child.* Belmont, CA: Fearon, 1972.

Fritz, Dorothy. *The Child and the Christian Faith.* Chicago, IL: Covenant, 1964.

Gordon, Ira. *The Infant Experience.* Columbus, OH: Merrill, 1975.

Haystead, Wesley. *You Can't Begin Too Soon.* Glendale, CA: G/L Publications, 1974.

Hildebrand, Verna. *Guiding Young Children.* New York: Macmillan, 1975.

Hirsch, Elisabeth, Ed. *The Block Book.* Washington, DC: National Association for the Education of Young Children, 1974.

Hymes, James. *Early Childhood Education: An Introduction to the Profession.* Washington, DC: National Association for the Education of Young Children, 1975.

Hymes, James. *Teaching the Child Under Six.* Columbus, OH: Merrill, 1968.

International Center for Learning Sunday School Teacher's Planbook: Early Childhood, Glendale, CA: G/L Publications, 1975.

Leeper, Sarah, et. al. *Good Schools for Young Children,* 3rd Edition, New York, NY: Macmillan, 1975.

McDaniel, Elsiebeth and Richards, Lawrence. *You and Preschoolers.* Chicago: Moody Press, 1975.

McDiarmid, Peterson and Sutherland. *Loving and Learning: Interacting with Your Child from Birth to Three.* New York, NY: Harcourt, Brace, Jovanovich, 1975.

Narramore, Bruce. *An Ounce of Prevention.* Grand Rapids, MI: Zondervan, 1973.

Nicholson, Dorothy. *Toward Effective Teaching.* Anderson, IN: Warner, 1970.

Pringle, Mia. *The Needs of Children.* New York: Schocken, 1975.

Read, Katherine. *The Nursery School: A Human Relationships Laboratory,* 5th Edition. Philadelphia, PA: Saunders, 1971.

Rickerson, Wayne. *Good Times for Your Family.* Glendale, CA: G/L Publications, 1976.

Wakefield, Norm. *You Can Have a Happier Family.* Glendale, CA: Gospel Light, 1977.

Willis, Anne and Ricciuti, Henry. *A Good Beginning for Babies: Guidelines for Group Care.* Washington, DC: National Association for the Education of Young Children, 1975.

Recipes

SALT-FLOUR DOUGH

Children enjoy the relaxation and unending variety of forms that come with molding, squeezing, rolling and pounding dough. This activity becomes even more fun when the children mix the dough themselves. Try these no-cook recipes for different textures:

Recipe No. 1
2 parts flour
1 part salt
1 tablespoon (15 ml) alum
Add water and dry tempera to achieve desired consistency and color.

Recipe No. 2
4 cups (1 l) flour
2 cups (.5 l) salt
food coloring
¼ cup (.06 l) salad oil
⅛ cup (.03 l) soap flakes
2 cups (.5 l) water
⅛ cup (.03 l) alum

Recipe No. 3
1½ cups (.375 l) flour
1 cup (.25 l) cornstarch
1 cup (.25 l) salt
1 cup (.25 l) warm water

Recipe No. 4 (Cooked)
  1 cup (.25 l) flour
  1 cup (.25 l) water and food coloring
  ½ cup (.125 l) salt
  1 tablespoon (15 ml) cooking oil
  2 teaspoons (10 ml) cream of tarter

Cook until consistency of mashed potatoes. Do not boil. Knead until cool.

With all recipes, if dough is sticky, dust with flour. If dough is stiff, add water. All recipes need to be stored in airtight containers. Recipe No. 3 hardens nicely and can be painted if sculptures are to be preserved.

PEANUT BUTTER CLAY
  Peanut butter
  Dry, powdered milk
  Honey

Mix equal parts peanut butter and powdered milk. Slowly add honey to achieve desired thickness. If mixture is too sticky, add more milk.

  Mold the "clay" into any desired shape. For added fun, decorate with seeds, raisins. Then, eat it!

HOMEMADE PAINT
  ½ cup (.125 l) vinegar
  ½ cup (.125 l) cornstarch
  Food coloring

Mix vinegar and cornstarch together. Add food coloring slowly as you stir, until desired color is reached. If paint is too thin add cornstarch. Add vinegar if too thick.

FINGER PAINT

Liquid starch
Soap flakes
Powdered tempera

Mix equal parts of starch and soap. Add tempera to achieve color desired. Add more starch if too thick, more soap if too thin.

FINGER WHIP

Soap flakes
Water
Beater

Mix equal parts water and soap flakes. Whip with beater. Add more water to thin, more soap to thicken.

PUD

½ box cornstarch
Water

Pour cornstarch onto shallow cookie tray. Add water slowly and stir. Pick it up. Squeeze it. Watch what happens!

HEALTHY SNACK IDEAS THAT CHILDREN CAN HELP PREPARE

Fresh fruit slices
Vegetable slices with dip
Banana dipped in sesame seeds
Cheese and crackers
Granola (try making your own)
Granola mixed with honey to make cookies
Fresh fruit salad
Sunflower seeds

Baked pumpkin seeds

Milk (mix equal parts whole milk with milk from powder to reduce cost)

Cereal mix (combine several dry cereals, mix with melted butter)

Fruit sandwich (fruit slices between crackers)

Yogurt (any flavor)

Stuffed celery (spread cream cheese or peanut butter, top with raisins or wheat germ)

Bible Time snack (mash dates, figs and raisins, form into balls, roll in graham cracker crumbs or wheat germ)

Yogurt milk shake (blend equal parts yogurt with fruit juice, plus some banana and honey for flavor)

Banana Delight (blend some banana, honey and ¼ teaspoon vanilla with milk—vary proportions to taste)